Leonard W. Levy is Andrew W. Mellon All-Claremont Professor of Humanities at the Claremont Graduate School, where he is also chairman of the Graduate Faculty of History. He won the Pulitzer Prize in History in 1969 for his book *Origins of the Fifth Amendment.* He is editor-in-chief of the four-volume *Encyclopedia of the American Constitution.* He has written and edited thirty books, among them *Emergence of a Free Press* and *Original Intent and the Framers' Constitution.*

JEFFERSON
& Civil Liberties

JEFFERSON
& Civil Liberties

THE DARKER SIDE

LEONARD W. LEVY

Elephant Paperbacks
Ivan R. Dee, Inc., Publisher, Chicago

◆ TO MY TEACHERS ◆

Henry Steele Commager

Felix Frankfurter

Max Lerner

First ELEPHANT PAPERBACK edition published 1989 by Ivan R. Dee, Inc., 1332 North Halsted Street, Chicago 60622. Manufactured in the United States of America.

Library of Congress Cataloging-in-Publication Data
Levy, Leonard Williams, 1923–
Jefferson & civil liberties.
Reprint. Originally published: Cambridge: Belknap Press of Harvard University Press, 1963.
Bibliography: p.
Includes index.
1. Civil rights—United States—History. 2. Jefferson, Thomas, 1743–1826—Views on civil rights. 3. United States—Politics and government—1789–1815. I. Title. II. Title: Jefferson and civil liberties.
KF4749.L484 1989 342.73'085'09 89-12019
ISBN 0-929587-11-1

PREFACE

Historians and biographers have fixed a libertarian halo around the brow of Thomas Jefferson as if he were a plaster saint, a seraph, or a demigod. That halo is, in part, the target of this book. Aiming at haloes is a destructive business. But a great teacher and democrat, Morris R. Cohen, on being reproached for his allegedly destructive criticism, used to reply: "You have heard the story of how Hercules cleaned the Augean stables. He took all the dirt and manure out and left them clean. You ask me, 'What did he leave in their stead?' I answer, 'Isn't it enough to have cleaned the stables?' " This book is a reflection of that spirit which I think is no more seditious, iconoclastic, or debunking than any scholarship that cares for truth and employs evidence responsibly.

Jefferson has been historically depicted as a noble figure caught in a mythic stance: swearing eternal hostility to every form of tyranny over the mind of man. Surprisingly, however, there has been no study of Jefferson and civil liberties. The focus of this study is the lesser known or "darker side" simply because Jefferson the apostle of liberty is so familiar a figure.

Focusing upon the darker side creates an unbalance that has the characteristics of a lawyer's brief or an indictment, although my presentation balances the conventional one. Nevertheless, balance has not been my objective for I see no need to construct for every page that calls a spade a spade an equal number of pages of conventional encomiums about the expounder of the rights of man. An indictment has certainly not been my objective either. I am now and have always been an admirer of Thomas Jefferson. But my admiration is tempered by a steely realism. I do not expect perfection from my political heroes; even the Greek gods had their faults.

Talking one way and acting another is not an uncommon trait among even the greatest American politicians. Time and circumstance sometimes alter their views. In Jefferson's case power produced a myopia that permitted bills of rights to be seen only dimly. Whether friend or foe was gored seems also to have made a difference to him. On occasion the compulsions to push through a program, despite its eroding effect on freedom, were irresistible. On still other occasions, when there was an awareness of libertarian claims, Jefferson found himself unable to serve them as he might wish; opposing pressures required compromise or surrender, particularly in time of danger, real or imagined.

Jefferson lived in a time of danger that he acutely apprehended—and exaggerated. It was a time of internal cold war in which the passionate exponents of the experiment in liberty felt besieged by its enemies, the defenders of an older order as well as the unscrupulous who sought to exploit every weakness of the new system. At such a time, Jefferson, the idealist come to power, did unto his enemies before they did unto him. Neither quite regarded the other as a legitimate opposition, equally loyal to the principles of the Republic.

Implicitly this book is a study of libertarian leadership in time of power and time of danger, as well as in a time when liberty itself was in its formative period. Contrary to the conventional version of American history, the first generation of independence did not bring liberty to its apogee; nor has it been eroding away ever since. But Jefferson, the foremost spokesman of that generation, voiced libertarian standards, though too shallow to prevail as more than rhetoric when pitted against the acid test of experience and crisis. My purpose, therefore, is mainly to depict the side of Jefferson that others have tended to neglect. I would agree with any critic that Jefferson should be seen as a whole man in the perspective of his times, just as Lincoln has been seen or as Wilson and Franklin Roosevelt are being seen. But the task of seeing Jefferson whole is for his biographers. Mine, in part, is to determine the validity of his historical reputation as the apostle of liberty.

Though I do not see him whole, I do see him as a figure of his time. If my judgments are often harsh, they are based on the standards of Jefferson's time, not on those of our own. That fact cannot be too strongly stressed. I have, for example, deliberately ignored the strain of racism in Jefferson's thought simply because he cannot be held responsible for having been born a white man in eighteenth century Virginia. On the other hand, the ban on general search warrants and the guarantee of freedom against unreasonable searches and seizures were well understood by the revolutionary generation that had lived with writs of assistance and insisted on the adoption of the Fourth Amendment. When, therefore, I find Jefferson palpably violating that amendment, I find him culpable or, as the more charitable might put it, inconsistent. Whether the issue is free press, fair trial, or intellectual liberty, I use "Jeffersonian" yardsticks. If they seem similar to those of our own time, the reason is simply that the civil-liberty cases encountered by Jefferson involved standards that had been well developed by or in his time.

How Jefferson gained his reputation as the central figure in the American libertarian tradition does not concern me. I address myself, rather, to the question whether he earned that reputation by his deeds as well as his words. I would strongly agree with anyone who contended that much of Jefferson was the best of his day and that the best of Jefferson was often the best of America. Much of the best was dreams and promises, but there was enough fulfillment as well as a stretching in the right direction to offset some of the evidence mustered here. In the case of Jefferson the apostle of liberty the whole may be larger than the sum of its parts, although I doubt it. It is the image, more than the reality, that has had the greatest influence. But my subject is the reality.

I find a strong pattern of unlibertarian, even antilibertarian thought and behavior extending throughout Jefferson's long career. It is a pattern that may distress his admirers, but it should be acknowledged, its significance weighed. Happily, freedom as a policy of practical wisdom constantly justifies itself. It has no need to rely upon authority, not even Jefferson's. He himself had little reverence for authority—or for haloes.

PREFACE TO THE PAPERBACK EDITION

The reappearance of this book will doubtless disappoint some critics who would prefer to see it evaporate into oblivion like a feculent odor. The criticisms that I received when the book was still in manuscript prepared me for the hostile reviews, though I had cherished the hope that the luck of the draw would give me a few more sympathetic reviewers than I got. I distributed copies of the manuscript to twenty readers. The original version, I should add, began at what is now page 15 with the story of the Roman soothsayers. With few exceptions the readers' reports did not coolly evaluate the evidence nor the conclusions based on it. Instead, most readers reacted as if I had engaged in a sort of secularized blasphemy, like desecration of the flag. They felt hurt and angry, as if they had a personal stake in Jefferson's reputation as the apostle of liberty and I had attacked an article of unquestionable faith. Several readers strongly objected to the very conception of the book—the presentation of just the "darker side" of Jefferson's record on civil liberties. Almost to a man they criticized me for lacking balance and writing an indictment or prosecutor's brief. The reports from friends, colleagues, and Jefferson-experts in the profession confirmed the subsequent prediction of the anonymous reader employed by the original publisher: "You'll get some furious reviews from the true believers."

The most revealing but least helpful reaction to the manuscript came in a letter from Julian P. Boyd, the one man, short of Dumas Malone, who was most qualified to give me criticism. After admitting that he had read only the concluding chapter—and my evidence is in the preceding chapters—he declared that he doubted whether he could ever bring himself to accept my point of view. He acknowledged being overly sympathetic to Jefferson and making uncritical judgments (though, in my opinion, Boyd's judgments are quite judicious). Yet he took the position, with which I cannot agree, that Jefferson cannot be measured except sympathetically and uncritically. He then alleged that my premises were unacceptable, my proofs unconvincing, and my standards often irrelevant and unfair. He concluded by declaring that if my view was right, he had wasted his best years in the wrong profession.

In my reply to Boyd I said that I would relish being proved wrong and would revise accordingly. I acknowledged that the book gave the impression of a *prima facie* case based on a prosecutor's brief, but pointed out that I candidly presented the darker side only and therefore did not deceive readers. I admitted that I might be unfair and stood correctable, but I questioned whether anyone should hold that my proofs were unconvincing without having examined them. I also tried to explain that my premises were those of a Jeffersonian libertarian. Above all, I solicited the full and careful reading of the manuscript that Boyd promised. He did not reply. I showed a copy of his letter to a friend who responded that he found it "a fascinating historical document. That he [Boyd] should have reacted as he did—without actually having read the manuscript—I think is an indication of the importance of bringing this material to light. His last sentence is a classic of its sort."

Although I refused to change the concept of the book, in deference to my critics I made some revisions, deleting some of the most objectionable adjectives to avoid the tone of an indictment. I also wrote a new beginning that was intended as a genuflection in the direction of the traditional Jefferson image so that the reader could be taken gently across familiar ground before being plunged into enemy territory. I also went out of my way in the preface to explain my purpose in focusing on the darker side, admitted that the book necessarily had the character of an indictment, as the subtitle openly suggested, and stressed that I was judging Jefferson on the civil liberties standards of his own time. When the book was published I sent a copy to Julian P. Boyd who replied that he would read it as soon as he could and give it his appraisal. Whatever the result, he graciously added, he was of the opinion that I had obligated all Jefferson scholars to re-examine their own attitudes and be prepared to defend them when challenged. Boyd never did provide an appraisal, but the reviewers certainly did. Their untarnishable belief in Jefferson was refreshing in a day when so many people believe in no god at all.

The most important review should have been that by Dumas Malone, the great Jefferson biographer, in the pages of the *American Historical Review*. He sent me a copy in advance of publication, saying that I would find that his main objection, like that of other Jeffersonians, was to the very conception of the book. I replied privately, as follows:

> I am returning the copy of the review of *Jefferson and Civil Liberties: The Darker Side,* that you were considerate enough to send me in advance of its publication. I guess we have reached the Mexican standoff that you anticipated when you remarked in a letter to me, "You did not expect me to like your book and I do not expect you to like my review, but you will understand that there is nothing personal in it." I suspect that

what divides us is the question whether personal likes or dislikes should have any bearing on historical scholarship. I think not and feel the same way toward your review; I neither like it nor dislike it, but believe it to be generally lacking in understanding, unfair, and misleading.

The review poorly reports the contents of the book and makes little effort to summarize any of the evidence relating to any of the subjects discussed. You do not inform readers, for example, that the book discusses the Josiah Philips case of attainder-and-outlawry, the problem of search-and-seizure under the Embargo acts, the bowdlerized edition of Hume, or a variety of other matters. To dismiss my seventy pages on the Burr conspiracy and the Embargo simply by remarking that my interpretation echoes that of Jefferson's contemporary political foes is to ignore entirely the specific civil liberties issues to which I address myself. I do not give a rap whether, for example, Burr was guilty. But I do care about the due process of law and fair trial issue, as well as about the difference between evidence that amounts to treason vs. constructive treason. My point generally is that you do not face up to the book, though you caricature it freely, and you don't explain to readers what I sought to do, however much I may have failed in the effort.

I object to your identification of me with Jefferson's political enemies. I am not now nor have I ever been a member of the Essex Junto, the Quids, the Burrites, or the Hamiltonians. I have much more respect for John Adams than you seem to have, but I regard myself as a "Jeffersonian," though I identify more closely with Madison or Gallatin than with Jefferson himself. In any case, it is quite misleading of you to leave reviewers with the impression that I write from a Federalist bias or judge Jefferson by Federalist criteria. That is simply not so. At other points in your review you seem uncertain about the criteria that I applied in reaching my judgments. I state again and again, and demonstrate, that I use the civil libertarian standards of Jefferson's own time as yardsticks to measure him.

For you to argue that Jefferson never set forth a systematic philosophy of free speech (we agree on this) because he "may have" doubted the feasibility of formulating one that would "always work," implies that he had thought through the issue. I challenge you to produce the evidence. Incidentally, if your abstract reasoning stands up, how do you explain the fact that Jefferson set forth a systematic philosophy in the case of freedom of religion? Surely he was neither doctrinaire nor unrealistic enough to think that his philosophy, more properly his overt-acts test, would "always" work.

Why should you wonder whether I approve of George Hay's proposition that free speech is either an absolute or does not exist? I make my views on that quite clear in [my earlier book] *Legacy of Suppression*. More significantly, you evade the real issue, which is whether the concept of seditious libel is consistent with free government. Gallatin and Madison, who were not "minor Republicans" (the validity of Hay's ideas does not depend on whether he was major or minor), repudiated the concept of seditious libel; Jefferson supported prosecutions for seditious libel by both the federal and state governments.

It simply will not do to evade hard problems by asserting that Jefferson was an absolutist with respect to freedom of mind and spirit. One's thoughts and feelings raise no issues until they find expression in words and deeds. The question then is where to draw the line between the permissible and the impermissible—and why. To speak of absolute freedom of the mind and spirit, unaccompanied by "free exercise," is a dodge and a sham. When in 1651 the Reverend John Clarke was convicted in Massachusetts for preaching Baptist doctrine, contrary to the law's prohibition, he was told, "The Court sentenced you not for your judgment or conscience, but for matter of fact and practice." In other words, the court acknowledged Clarke's freedom of mind and spirit. Yet he replied, "Be it so, but I say that matter of fact and practice was but the manifestation of my judgment and conscience; and I make account that man is void of judgment and conscience, with respect unto God, that hath not a fact and practice suitable thereunto." Jefferson would have agreed and, accordingly, devised the "overt-acts" test to protect the expression of religious opinion. What is significant is his failure to extend that test to political opinion. The "new libertarianism" advocated the overt-acts test for political as well as religious opinions. Your association of the new libertarianism with Hay's absolutist views, and exoneration of Jefferson as no absolutist except as to freedom of mind and spirit, will fool no one.

It seems to me that you have your cake and eat it too by the proposition that on the one hand Jefferson was a great champion of personal liberties but on the other was a "relativist" deserving our praise. When he defends liberty, you approve; when he doesn't, you approve and praise him for not being doctrinaire, not being absolutist, indeed for being relativist. On what principle do you make the distinction? More important, on what principle did he make the distinction? I cannot accept your standard of judgment, namely that on balance he was more libertarian than his enemies. I should not like to think that Pickering or Ames set the standards by which we judge Jefferson.

I suppose that I may have earned the tinge of sarcasm in your first page, for I probably overstated my case, though some have thought that I am too defensive and apologetic. But you ignore the case altogether, leaving the impression—to me a humorous one—that I have written a faintly dirty book. You make far too much of and distort a reference in the preface to a classic metaphor about the Augean stables. Indeed you give more attention to the first page of my preface than to several chapters of the book. I am mystified why you should regard as dirt indisputable evidence that proves the existence of Jefferson's darker side on questions of civil liberty. Incidentally, the metaphor refers to cleaning, not dirtying, the stables.

Malone was right about one point. He hoped that I would find nothing objectionable in the tone of his review, and I didn't. I did think that quite a few reviews, including some from the liberal establishment, were nasty or malicious as well as unfair and misleading. David Fellman, an eminent constitutional scholar who was president of the American Association of University Professors and an officer of the American Civil Liberties Union, dismissed the book summarily by saying in the pages of the *Progressive* that I sustained my thesis only by overstretching the evidence, though he gave no particulars. He concluded:

> Thus, in his long discussion of Jefferson's handling of the embargo, about all Levy proves is that Jefferson had a hard time enforcing a difficult (and probably unwise) policy to which he was strongly committed. Much of this book, I am afraid, strikes me as pretty small beer.

I had thought that civil libertarians, going back to James Otis's time, regarded unreasonable searches and seizures as rating at least a jeroboam of beer. In *Civil Liberties,* the monthly publication of the ACLU, Louis M. Hacker judged the book on the basis of whether it would be "of much help in furthering the cause of civil liberties," an instrumentalist use of history which, like any political considerations or present-mindedness, I always regard as an enemy of scholarship. Hacker managed, like Fellman, to slip in a line about the "dubious validity" of "some" of my evidence, without giving any examples. In the *Washington Post* the book was reviewed by Alan Barth, author of several excellent volumes defending civil liberties and an editorialist for the newspaper. The gist of his review reappeared in the editorial page of the same newspaper in 1967 after President Johnson had appointed me a member of the American Revolution Bicentennial Commission. Under the heading "Subcommittee on Warts" appeared these words:

> There will be, as is always the case, criticism of some of the members, and praise for others. Some will be surprised to find on the commission Dr. Leonard W. Levy whose views of Thomas Jefferson and some other aspects of the period would suggest that he hardly thought the occasion [of the nation's bicentennial] worth celebrating. Of his book on Jefferson, published in 1963, this newspaper's reviewer said: "The book presents a mass of material, no doubt painstakingly researched, to support these charges. The result is not merely an unbalanced portrait; it is a gargoyle. It is all very well to paint a

man, as Cromwell put it, warts and all; but if one paints the warts alone, one has very little picture of the man. . . . The recitation of every misstep in Jefferson's life, including even gossip about an amatory dalliance,* is so hostile that one reacts to it as one would to scandalmongering about a friend." Fortunately, Mr. Levy is only one member of a large commission. The chairman might well assign him to the subcommittee on warts and leave the rest of the commission the task of commemorating the constructive side of the statesmen of the revolution.

In *Book Week,* the book review section of the now defunct *New York Herald Tribune,* which syndicated *Book Week* in other newspapers in the country, Alpheus T. Mason, one of the foremost constitutional scholars of our time, stated, "Searing indictments crowd almost every page." Ignoring my discussion of Jefferson's failures as a libertarian theorist, Mason confidently but without any evidence observed that, "As a libertarian theorist, Jefferson is without a peer." The review concluded with a *tu quoque* which I took as a private joke, almost as amusing as the editorial on warts. Said Mason:

> Emerson cautioned the youthful Oliver Wendell Holmes jr., "When you strike at a king, you must kill him." Mr. Levy makes the apocalyptic halo around Jefferson the target of his book. The giant of American liberalism still survives.

In 1957, reviewing Mason's book on Harlan Fiske Stone in the *American Historical Review,* I wrote that to justify Stone's views the author made Charles Evans Hughes the villain of the book and even disparaged Holmes and Brandeis in order to elevate Stone's stature. "Mason's thrusts at Hughes," I declared, "recall to mind the injunction: 'When you strike at a king you must kill him.' "

*See page 65 for my presentation of the "gossip."

Cecelia Kenyon, the author of several brilliant essays on politics during Jefferson's time, wrote the only review of the book that purported to challenge my evidence as well as my interpretation. Eric McKitrick said of me, in his *Commentary* review, that I had used "blunt words and blunt facts" in an "implacable, injudicious, indispensable book." When I read Kenyon's review I was shocked by the blunt words and what seemed to be blunt facts, as well as an implacable hostility. I suppose she treated me as she thought I had treated Jefferson. Unable to believe that I had been guilty of so many distortions, I was forced by her review to compare what I had said with what she attributed to me. As a result I felt compelled to answer publicly in the pages of the *New York Review of Books.* In a letter to the editors, I wrote:

> I write to protest the outrageously inaccurate and deceiving review of my book, *Jefferson and Civil Liberties: The Darker Side,* by Cecelia Kenyon in the November 14 issue. She falsely says that I "give the impression that Jefferson meant to foist off upon some unsuspecting student a politically bowdlerized edition of Hume. . . ." Yet I show that Jefferson candidly told a student that Hume was full of "errors and heresies" and that the student should read, instead, a book by Baxter who had changed Hume's text. She claims that Jefferson did not engage in intellectual deception, because he wanted Hume's name on the title page and I am chastised for not having said so. I said so; he wanted the book called "Hume's history republicanized." That fact increases rather than diminishes the deception, for Jefferson did want readers to think that they were reading Hume. Baxter's politically bowdlerized version appealed to him because readers couldn't tell where Hume's text had been altered. The deception had to do with the text itself, not just the title page. The important point is that Jefferson didn't trust readers to be exposed to the original Hume, nor follow his own maxim that truth will best falsehood in a fair encounter.

Miss Kenyon seeks to dissociate Jefferson from a statute of Virginia abridging freedom of political expression. She says that I associate Jefferson with the statute because he signed it as governor but do not take note of the fact that the governor had no veto power. The reader of her review will not know that the statute was a reenactment of one passed four years earlier when Jefferson was the chief draftsman of Virginia's legislation; that it was a companion piece to a bill on treason, passed simultaneously, that he did write; that while he could not veto the bill when governor, he was free to criticize it and did not; that if he did not wish to criticize it when in office, he was free to do so in his *Notes on Virginia,* written shortly after leaving the governorship; that he criticized other legislation in the *Notes on Virginia,* but not this; that he did not do so because when he was governor, he used the statute to imprison persons, against whom there was admittedly no legal evidence, suspected as disaffected individuals who might aid the enemy at some future time.

Miss Kenyon attacks me on the matter of the wartime loyalty oath. She doesn't doubt that Jefferson supported the oath, but argues, curiously, that it was philosophically justified by the Declaration of Independence. I wouldn't so malign Jefferson. I do not ignore the fact that the oath was intended to engender support of a revolutionary government, and I do not treat it as if it were similar to current loyalty oaths. Miss Kenyon gives the false impression that it was an innocuous oath, like an oath of allegiance or a naturalization oath. It was, rather, a test oath whose purpose was to identify persons whom Jefferson called traitors "in thought, but not in deed." Naturalization oaths were not required of citizens even in the eighteenth century and did not punish belief or impose upon nonjurors penalties denying them liberty and property without due process of law as did this oath.

Miss Kenyon ridicules my treatment of Jefferson's use of the army during the Embargo era, as if there were no validity at that time to Jefferson's principle that a standing army in time of peace menaced public and personal liberty. He and his followers thought so and argued that point, with proof to spare, right up to the time Jefferson resorted to the extra-legal use of the army. My reviewer contends that if Jefferson used the army against his own people, it must have been all right because Eisenhower and Kennedy did the same. They, however, were enforcing the law of land as judicially determined, while Jefferson's authority was dubious. But comparisons with the present are beside the point. Jefferson must be judged by the laws and standards of his own time. The only relevant comparisons must be with Washington and Adams who used troops to suppress the Whiskey and Fries Rebellions. Both scrupulously followed the letter of the law; acted, as Jefferson did not, in support of the judiciary to buttress, not bypass, civil authority; and quickly withdrew the troops. Jefferson used the military as an occupation force for months at a time, ignoring, defying, or circumventing the federal courts and the law. He finally got a drastic force act henceforth legalizing his routine military enforcement of the laws against American citizens.

Miss Kenyon claims that I take for granted both the success of the Revolution and the continued durability of the republican experiment, whereas Jefferson realized that the experiment was a novel one whose outcome was uncertain—something that I allegedly cannot conceive. That is false. I not only conceive of, understand, and appreciate this view, but elaborate on it in the first and last chapters and even refer to it in the preface. I wish that space permitted me to quote pages 22–24 in particular as proof that Miss Kenyon has a casual regard for truth. Indeed, I use the point that "Men did not then take for granted that the new nation would survive" (p. 23) somewhat sympathetically as my chief explanation of Jefferson's "darker side."

As for my alleged use of today's standards to judge Jefferson, I reiterate in the book that he can be judged only by the standards of his time, and I try my best to judge him that way. My reviewer uses contemporary standards or models and then accuses me of being present-minded. On bills of attainder and outlawry, on constructive treason, on search and seizure, on fair trial and due process, on the scope and meaning of freedom of the press, on prescription of textbooks or proscription of political heresies among students, I state and use the standards of Jefferson's time.

Finally, I welcome Miss Kenyon's admissions that Jefferson was not overscrupulous with respect to judicial procedures; played fast and loose with the Constitution, especially with the guarantee against unreasonable searches and seizures; and supported—though not "very vigorously" (that's funny)—state (and federal) prosecutions for seditious libel, that is, for criticism of his Administration. For him to have supported such prosecutions at all, after the Sedition Act stink, after men in his own party had developed a broad new theory of a free press that repudiated altogether the concept of seditious libel, suggests that the apostle of liberty had a darker side.

Most of this letter was published with a rejoinder by Miss Kenyon that I regarded almost as misleading as her original review. She did, however, catch me in an important error of omission when she declared that I failed to report that Jefferson had an alternative suggestion for dealing with Hume. He recommended at one point that Hume's entire text be reprinted with contrary statements from others placed in collateral columns or in notes. Miss Kenyon was also correct when she suggested that I should have considered Jefferson's recommendation for the bowdlerized version in the context of then prevailing practices related to literary plagiarism and piracy. On the matter of Jefferson's relation to the state act abridging freedom of expression, she accused me of building a case of guilt by association and of failing to compare the two versions of the act, though I did not fail to do so. She thought that my description of Jefferson's use of the army to enforce the Embargo Acts was exaggerated, and ignoring my comparison of the use of the army by Jefferson's predecessors, she alleged that I hold the dubious belief that a President may execute only such laws as are subjected to prior judicial validation. She continued to insist that I failed to stress the crises of Jefferson's time. The main point of her rejoinder dealt with the problem of standards. She acknowledged that I made "an attempt to apply those of Jefferson's time," but claimed that I failed. "I would qualify my original statement, however," she added, "by excluding from my conclusion the treatment of some of the procedural liberties." She then alleged that I appeared to follow modern standards based on hindsight, and she disagreed with my statement that the "standards themselves had been established" in Jefferson's time. Tartly she concluded that my standards for judging Jefferson "are predominantly those of a modern and doctrinaire libertarianism."

The same theme about my misuse of standards appeared in several other reviews. Marshall Smelser in the *Review of Politics* declared, "Levy is, *in detail,* correct." He granted, as he put it, that Jefferson would not be eligible for membership in the ACLU. The trouble with the book, Smelser found, was that I did not understand that Jefferson was "a seventeenth-century politician and a tenth-century lawyer, and he always behaved so." Ignoring Jefferson's warning about the tyranny of the legislature, Smelser declared that to Jefferson the acts of the legislature expressed the whole people. "If seventeenth-century whig idols passed acts of attainder, Jefferson could write an act of attainder. He could also approve of the idea of a process of outlawry. . . ." Smelser also stated, "Mr. Levy says every liberal precedent Jefferson needed in order to do the Decent Thing could be found in the history of seventeenth-century England." I said no such thing, but his point was that the standards by which I judge Jefferson were not fixed in his own time. Donald G. Morgan made the point more persuasively in a sympathetic review in the *Journal of Southern History* when he noted, "After all, the best standards of enlightened leaders in calmer moments are hardly identical with prevailing standards."

David H. Fischer, in his book *Historians' Fallacies,* working a similar theme, argued that I had committed an analytical fallacy of anachronism "of serious proportions." In an utterly wrong and perverse passage, he concluded his criticism as follows:

> Levy formed in his own mind an idea of what civil liberties *should* entail—an idea which has *some* relevance in *some* of its particulars to *some* of Jefferson's associates (men younger than Jefferson himself). Then he proceeded to condemn Jefferson, sometimes explicitly, sometimes by innuendo, for not living up to this exalted atemporal standard. In short, Levy analyzed and evaluated Jefferson by measuring his acts and attitudes against the standards of the ACLU and tallying all the discrepancies. The result is objectionable not merely because it is unfair to Jefferson but also because it distorts and falsifies the texture of Jeffersonian thought.

In a devastating essay on Fischer's book, Louis O. Mink, in *History and Theory,* wrote:

> An example of grammatical misinterpretation is Fischer's identification as a "fallacy of anachronism" the statement by Leonard Levy in his book on Jefferson (133–134) that "during Jefferson's lifetime, there was never an issue for which incontestably familiar libertarian standards were lacking to guide his judgment." This, Fischer says, is "a very great mistake on Levy's part. It is factually false . . . "—because there were in that era *different* ideas of liberty which were contestable and contested. But this reply is *ignoratio elenchi* [ignorant refutation, or the fallacy of irrelevance]. Fischer's statement, if true, disproves the claim that there were *familiar incontestable standards,* but not Levy's actual statement that there were *incontestably familiar standards* (which leaves open the possibility that there were different standards, all familiar to Jefferson). Maybe Levy *meant* to say that standards were incontestable, but that is not what he *did* say, nor does Fischer

seem to notice that what he repudiates is not Levy's statement as quoted.

I shall in the future return to the subject of Jefferson and civil liberties to expand and revise the book, clarifying incontestably the whole issue of standards, explaining them in detail and treating the whole of Jefferson, not just the darker side. For the time being, however, I like to think that there is more to the present version than my daughter, Leslie, has seen in it. On a recent trip to the national capital, we visited the Jeffersonian Memorial at night when the impressive statue of Jefferson was brightly lit from the front view only. She circled round to the back and remarked, "Now I see what you meant by the darker side of Jefferson." Others have seen more than that in the book and have been able to read it without emotional loss of their celestial equanimity. Chief Justice Earl Warren found it both fascinating and enjoyable. "We sometimes forget," he wrote me, "the complex development of men of history as we accept them, and I was extremely interested in reading this penetrating analysis of one of our greatest. It also reminds us that while they, like the rest of us, have feet of clay, their hearts or minds often take them where their feet would not support them." Arthur M. Schlesinger, also in a private letter, wrote of the book that it is a "perspicuous, realistic exposition of the subject which explains much that has hitherto been misunderstood about Jefferson and also his times. I learned a great deal from it. For example, I had never quite faced up to Jefferson's conduct of the Burr affair or to his management of the embargo. My chief criticism of the book is that I think you are needlessly defensive in the preface and the first chapter as to your aim." The main question that I shall have to confront, when the time comes for a revision of the book, is whether the darker side of Jefferson is really outweighed by a consideration of his whole record on civil liberties.

Leonard W. Levy

Claremont, California
April 1972

CONTENTS

JEFFERSON

& Civil Liberties

✧ Chapter One ✧

The Jefferson Image

ALTHOUGH history can be quoted to support any cause, just as scripture can be quoted by the devil, no wrenching of the past can alter a transcending fact about Thomas Jefferson: he believed in the right and capacity of the ordinary man to live responsibly in freedom. Lincoln testified for the ages that the principles of Jefferson were "the definitions and axioms of free society."[1] It is Jefferson, if not Lincoln himself, who is the central figure in the history of American democracy. Fervently did he believe, fondly did he conceive, that the will and welfare of the people were the only prop and purpose of government. Others pitted liberty and equality against each other as if a tension, even a contradiction, existed between them. To Jefferson, liberty and equality were complementary qualities of the condition to which man had a moral right. He suffused the Declaration of Independence with an ethical philosophy—not merely a political or legal one—that permanently nourished the American spirit.

Jefferson's principles sprang from the deepest aspirations of the people. A communion of sentiment tied him to them, despite his tendency to shrink from too close a personal contact. He expressed himself in literary utterance that was a model of clarity and beauty—understandable, appealing, and almost unfailingly humane. With crisp eloquence he memorably voiced the noblest hopes for human fortune on earth. In so doing, he somehow illuminated the lives of his compatriots—their needs, their best values, their ambitions. His deepest sympathies belonged to the disadvantaged and downtrodden; his deepest trust was in the power of his fellow men to do justice and to fulfill themselves on their own terms, self-reliant and self-governing, as long as they had the opportunity to make informed, unfettered choices; his deepest faith was in the emancipating effect of education and freedom on the human personality. His confidence in popular government, bounded only by respect for minority rights, was anchored in a belief that counting heads was a much better way to rule than breaking them. It secured sounder policies, more beneficial to the general welfare, than those determined by the privileged few.

Jefferson "still survives," to quote the famous deathbed words of John Adams, because a free people still cherishes the spirit of liberty and its foremost exponent among the founders of the Republic. Jefferson hated tyranny and war, poverty and privilege, bigotry and ignorance; he hated whatever crippled man's spirit or body. His influence was zealously devoted to securing the conditions of freedom which would make possible the "pursuit of happiness" by all. He championed free public education and attacked the aristocratic system of entail and primogeniture. He condemned slavery and recommended its gradual abolition. He reformed the criminal code of his state, and tightened the constitutional definition of treason to prevent the use of the criminal law as an instrument of political oppression. He advocated freedom of the press and resisted the noxious Alien and Sedition Acts. He insisted on the subordination of the military to the civil authority. He converted Madison to the cause of adding a Bill of Rights to the new federal Constitution. He supported a broadening of the base of popular government by public-land grants that would enable every citizen to meet the property qualification on the right to vote. Almost always Jefferson's impulses were generous and liberating. And on some matters, like religious liberty, he displayed a principled consistency.

No great crimes like the Inquisition or Saint Bartholomew's Eve Massacre drenched the pages of its history with the blood of dissenters, but "persecution for the cause of conscience" was a frequent menace in early America. On the eve of the Revolution, for example, Baptists lay in Virginia's jails for publishing their religious sentiments, and James Madison heatedly cried out that the "diabolical Hell conceived principle of persecution rages."[2] Priests were threatened with death or imprisonment; heresy laws made certain religious opinions criminal; and the Church of England was legally established in Virginia. The establishment permitted only its clergy to solemnize marriages, required attendance at its services, and taxed the entire population for its support.[3] Jefferson and Madison, in a magnificent collaboration, championed the cause of the dissenters. They led a ten-year battle—the severest, said

Jefferson, in which he had ever engaged—culminating in a victory for the free exercise of religion and separation of church and state.

Jefferson believed, as did Roger Williams, that "compulsion stincks in God's nostrils." Toleration was only less repugnant; a mere point of midpassage from persecution to liberty, toleration at its best—when it implied no enforced tithes or civil disabilities—was in Jefferson's opinion merely a concession from the state, a privilege granted but revocable. He believed that religion was a private duty which free men owed their Creator. The manner of discharging that duty was none of the state's business. It was, rather, an unquestionable and illimitable natural right, to be exercised freely according to the dictates of conscience. Thanks to Madison, who took the lead in Williamsburg while Jefferson served in the Continental Congress, the proposed Virginia Bill of Rights was amended to guarantee that all men were "equally entitled to the free exercise of religion," not just to "the fullest toleration."[4]

It remained for Jefferson to draft the implementing legislation that made the new constitutional principle an operating reality. Back in Williamsburg for the October session of the legislature in 1776, he introduced legislation that would have systematically destroyed the establishment. He succeeded only in part, losing on the main issue of the relation of church and state. The legislature adopted his proposals for the repeal of all laws punishing any religious opinions or modes of worship. Dissenters were exempted from compulsory support of the Church of England, and state taxation on its behalf was postponed. The legislature, however, reserved for future decision the question whether religion ought to be supported on a nonpreferential basis by a new establishment in which all denominations would share.[5]

In 1779 Patrick Henry introduced a General Assessment Bill predicated on the supposition, expressed in its preamble, that the state must encourage religion. This bill stipulated that the Christian religion should be "the established religion." Each denomination was to share the tax proceeds; every person was to designate the church of his membership which alone would receive his taxes. Money collected from persons not designating membership was to be divided proportionately among the churches of their county.[6] Henry's bill created a plural or multiple establishment of religion.

Plural establishments existed at the time in six other states—Massachusetts, New Hampshire, Connecticut, Maryland, South Carolina, and Georgia, the only ones which maintained or authorized any establishments after the Revolution.[7] In each, as in the proposed system for Virginia, there was no single state church. The concept of an establishment in America meant government aid and sponsorship of religion generally. By contrast, in every European precedent, as in colonial Virginia, it had meant the preference of one church over all others. In post-Revolutionary America the government's impartial or nonpreferential support—principally tax support—of religion or of religious institutions had become the only form of establishment. All churches in a plural or American establishment were equal before the law.

The rhetoric of religious freedom and equalitarianism was employed to defend the liberalized establishment proposed by Patrick Henry, with the backing of George Washington, Edmund Randolph, and Richard

Henry Lee. Henry's plan also had a politically seductive charm: by taking in the dissenters, it bought off the opposition. Jefferson, however, countered with a plan which revealed the specious quality of the argument in behalf of plural establishments. His Bill for Establishing Religious Freedom, a classic expression of the American creed on intellectual as well as religious liberty was, indeed, a fulfillment of the philosophy of the Declaration of Independence. Beginning with the announcement that "Almighty God hath created the mind free, and manifested his supreme will that free it shall remain by making it altogether insusceptible of restraint," Jefferson elaborated on his theme that religion was a private, voluntary matter of individual conscience beyond the scope of the civil power to support or restrain. The preamble concluded:

> that to suffer the civil magistrate to intrude his powers into the field of opinion and to restrain the profession or propagation of principles on supposition of their ill tendency is a dangerous falacy [*sic*], which at once destroys all religious liberty, because he being of course judge of that tendency will make his opinions the rule of judgment, and approve or condemn the sentiments of others only as they shall square with or differ from his own; that it is time enough for the rightful purposes of civil government for its officers to interfere when principles break out into overt acts against peace and good order; and finally, that truth is great and will prevail if left to herself; that she is the proper and sufficient antagonist to error, and has nothing to fear from the conflict unless by human interposition disarmed of her natural weapons, free argument and debate; errors ceasing to be dangerous when it is permitted freely to contradict them.

The next section of the bill provided that no man should be compelled to frequent or support any worship whatever, nor be restrained in any way on account of his religious opinions.[8]

The Virginia legislature, confronted by diametrically opposed bills—Jefferson's complete separation of religion and government against Henry's plural establishment—remained deadlocked until after Jefferson sailed for France in 1784. In the following year, thanks to Madison's masterful political tactics and his famous "Memorial and Remonstrance against Religious Assessments," the legislature passed Jefferson's bill.[9] Jefferson's pride of authorship was so great that he ranked the bill with the Declaration of Independence as contributions for which he most wanted to be remembered.

Jefferson faithfully adhered to the principles of his bill throughout his life. On innumerable occasions he reiterated them and, more significantly, put them into practice. As President, for example, he departed from the precedents of Washington and Adams by refusing to recommend or designate any day for national prayer, fasting, or thanksgiving. Civil powers alone, he insisted, were vested in the President of the United States; he therefore possessed no authority to direct or even recommend exercises of a religious character. To do so would in his opinion constitute an establishment of religion, in violation of the First Amendment.[10] Only a totally principled commitment to the privacy and voluntary nature of religious belief explained so exquisite a constitutional conscience.

Jefferson's most quoted presidential statement on the subject appeared in his letter to the Baptist Association of Danbury, Connecticut. Declaring that religion was "solely between man and his God," he added: "I contemplate with sovereign reverence that act of the whole

American people which declared that their legislature should 'make no law respecting an establishment of religion, or prohibiting the free exercise thereof,' thus building a wall of separation between church and state."[11] The Danbury letter was not a "little address of courtesy" containing a "figure of speech."[12] Nor was it "motivated by an impish desire to heave a brick at the Congregationalist-Federalist hierarchy of Connecticut."[13] Jefferson had powerful convictions on the subject of religious liberty which he always approached most solemnly.

While writing this letter he was so concerned with the necessity of expressing himself with deliberation and care that he sought the approbation of the attorney general, explaining: "Averse to receive addresses, yet unable to prevent them, I have generally endeavored to turn them to some account, by making them the occasion, by way of answer, of sowing useful truths and principles among the people, which might germinate and become rooted among their political tenets. The Baptist address, now enclosed, admits of a condemnation of the alliance between Church and State, under the authority of the Constitution. It furnishes an occasion, too, which I have long wished to find, of saying why I do not proclaim fastings and thanksgivings, as my predecessors did."[14]

Jefferson's consistency in applying the principle of the separation of church and state was also evident in the field of education. It has been contended that he advocated the use of public funds in Virginia for a school of theology for the training of clergymen; that he approved of elaborate arrangements for the students of private theological schools to share the facilities of the University of Virginia; that he recommended that a room in the university be used for worship; and that he did not protest against the use by Virginia of tax monies on behalf of religious education. It has been contended, in other words, that his principle of total separation was not put into practice.[15]

In matters of education, however, Jefferson was a complete secularist, never deviating in any significant degree. In 1778 he submitted, in a Bill for the More General Diffusion of Knowledge, a comprehensive plan for public education at the primary and secondary levels.[16] Religious instruction was completely absent from the proposed curriculum at a time when it was a prominent feature in schools everywhere else. The omission was deliberate; Jefferson wrote in his *Notes on the State of Virginia:* "Instead therefore of putting the Bible and Testament into the hands of the children, at an age when their judgments are not sufficiently matured for religious enquiries, their memories may here be stored with the most useful facts from Grecian, Roman, European and American history."[17] Religion was also conspicuous by its absence from Jefferson's plan of 1817; his Bill for Establishing a System of Public Education enumerated only secular subjects. In an effort to eliminate possible religious influence in the public schools, Jefferson specified that ministers should not serve as "visitors" or supervisors, and provided that "no religious reading, instruction or exercise, shall be prescribed or practised" in violation of the tenets of any sect or denomination.[18] Clearly, Jefferson opposed the use of public funds for the teaching of religion in the public schools.

Jefferson's first proposal on higher education came in

1779. His Bill for the Amending of the Constitution of the College of William and Mary stated that the college consisted of "one school of sacred theology, with two professorships therein, to wit, one for teaching the Hebrew tongue, and expounding the holy scriptures; and the other for explaining the commonplaces of divinity, and controversies with heretics." There were six other professorships divided among a school of philosophy, one of classical languages, and another for teaching Indians reading, writing, and "the catechism and the principles of the Christian religion." Jefferson proposed to abolish both the school of theology with its professorships of religion and the school for teaching Indians. In place of the school for Indians he proposed that a missionary be selected by a newly constituted faculty who would not teach religion but investigate Indian "laws, customs, religions, traditions, and more particularly their languages." Jefferson's missionary was to be an anthropologist charged with reporting his findings to the faculty and preserving his reports in the college library. In place of the school of theology and the professorships of religion, Jefferson proposed simply a professorship "of moral philosophy" and another "of history, civil and ecclesiastical."[19]

Jefferson's proposed bill failed because of Episcopalian opposition. However, in the same year, 1779, he and Madison as visitors of the college instituted such changes as could be made by executive authority without legislative approval. In 1821 he summarized the changes by writing: "When I was a visitor, in 1779, I got the two professorships of Divinity . . . put down, and others of law and police, of medicine, anatomy, and chemistry, and of modern languages substituted."[20] A comparable statement appeared in his *Notes on the State of Virginia* where he remarked that the school of divinity was "excluded."[21]

Jefferson was never satisfied with the education offered by the College of William and Mary. Failing to achieve adequate reform of the college, he turned to the establishment of a new state university. He also attempted in 1814 to transform Albemarle Academy, a small private school. He wanted an enlarged institution, offering instruction from the primary grades through college and post-graduate training, that would be supported in part by public funds. At no point in the entire curriculum before the professional level was there any provision for religious education. However, one of the "professional schools" was to be devoted to "Theology and Ecclesiastical History," to which would come the "ecclesiastic" as would the "lawyer to the school of law."[22] Here is an inconsistency, indicating Jefferson's support of the use of tax monies on behalf of religious education, although only at the graduate level. It is not irrelevant to stress, however, that Albemarle was privately established and endowed, though it was to be aided by public funds. More to the point is the fact that never again, after the failure of this proposal, did Jefferson renew it.

In 1818, for instance, his academic plan for the newly authorized state university included ten professorships and thirty-four subjects, none of them relating to religion. This curriculum, which was adopted, was laid out in a report, written by Jefferson as chairman of the commissioners for the University of Virginia, which stated: "In conformity with the principles of our Constitution, which places all sects of religion on an equal footing . . . we have proposed no professor of divinity . . .

Proceeding thus far without offence to the Constitution, we have thought it proper at this point to leave every sect to provide, as they think fittest, the means of further instruction in their own peculiar tenets." The report also stated: "It is supposed probable, that a building . . . may be called for in time, in which may be rooms for religious worship . . . for public examinations, for a library."[23] The very conditional phrasing of this sentence suggests that Jefferson was seeking to fend off an anticipated barrage of criticism against the university as a "godless" institution. In fact he was under constant pressure from church groups to make suitable provision for theological training and religious worship at the university. The "supposed probable" room which might in time be a place for worship was a concession to those, who, as Jefferson reported in a letter to Dr. Thomas Cooper, used the absence of a professorship of divinity to spread the idea that the university was "not merely of no religion, but against all religion."[24]

Opposition to the secular character of the university resulted in a postponement of instruction, forcing additional concessions to religious interests. In 1822 Jefferson, as rector of the university, and the Board of Visitors, among them Madison, proposed in the most reluctant language to accept a suggestion "by some pious individuals . . . to establish their religious schools on the confines of the University, so as to give their students ready and convenient access and attendance on the scientific lectures of the University." This report noted also that the religious schools would offer places where regular students of the university could worship as they pleased, "But always understanding that these schools shall be independent of the University and of each other." The report concluded that if the legislature questioned "what here is suggested, the idea will be relinquished on any surmise of disapprobation which they might think proper to express."[25] The legislature did not, however, take the eager hint to scrap the plan which involved no public expense.

Jefferson explained that in order to silence the calumny that the university was atheistic, "In our annual report to the legislature, after stating the constitutional reasons against a public establishment of any religious instruction, we suggest the expediency of encouraging the different religious sects to establish, each for itself, a professorship of their own tenets, on the confines of the University."[26] In 1824, shortly before the first classes, Jefferson and the Board of Visitors adopted formal regulations which provided that the "religious sects of this State" might "establish within, or adjacent to, the precincts of the University, schools for instruction in the religion of their own sect." Students of the university were "free, and expected to attend religious worship" at the "establishment" of their choice on condition that they did so in the mornings before classes, which began at 7:30 A.M. The same regulations also provided for the use of one of the university's rooms for worship as well as for other purposes, although the students were enjoined by the regulation of the previous paragraph to attend services in the theological seminaries surrounding the university.[27]

No part of the regular school day was set aside for religious worship. Possibly the proposal that a room belonging to the university be used for worship was intended originally as a makeshift arrangement until the various sects established their own schools of theology.

None in fact did so for several decades, and Jefferson did not permit the room belonging to the university to be used for religious purposes. In 1825 he rejected a proposal to hold Sunday services on university property. The Board of Visitors, he wrote, had already turned down an application to permit a sermon to be preached in one of the rooms on the ground that "the buildings of the Univ. belong to the state, that they were erected for the purposes of an Univ., and that the Visitors, to whose care they are commd [commanded or committed] for those purposes, have no right to permit their application to any other." His position was that the legislature had failed to sanction a proposal to use university facilities for worship and that, consequently, an alternative plan had been adopted *"superseding* the 1st idea of permitting a room in the Rotunda to be used for religious worship."[28] The alternative plan was the one permitting the different sects to establish their own divinity schools, without public aid, independently of the university. The university did not even appoint a chaplain while Jefferson was its rector. "At a time when, in most colleges and universities of the country, ministers were presidents and common members of boards of control, daily chapel attendance was compulsory, courses in religion were required, and professors of theology and doctors of divinity had a prominent place on the faculties, the University of Virginia stood out sharply in contrast with its loyalty to the principle of separation of church and state."[29]

Jefferson cared very deeply about religious liberty. Diligent study and thought had given him a systematic theory, the most advanced of his age, and he put it into practice. His position was clearly defined, publicly stated, and vigorously defended. Although it exposed him to abusive criticism he carried on his fight for separation of church and state, and for the free exercise of religion, throughout his long public career without significant contradictions. In sum his thought on religious liberty was profoundly libertarian, and his actions suited his thought.

However, Jefferson's ideas on many other issues were not always libertarian; and when they were his practice did not always match his professions. Between his words and deeds on religious liberty there was an almost perfect congruence, but it was not a congruence that was characteristic.

There is a story about two Roman soothsayers whose job was to edify the populace with prophecies that were intended to sustain the ancient faith. While solemnly examining the entrails of an ox for signs and portents, they winked at each other. Historians who perpetuate an idealized image of Jefferson should be no less realistic about their own craft. A realism more in keeping with Jefferson's spirit would not depict him as a plaster saint of faultless civil libertarian virtues. William James once wrote that the notion of God's omnipotence must be relinquished if God is to be kept as a religious object, because the only God worthy of the name must be finite. Similarly the notion of Jefferson's perfection as a libertarian must be relinquished if he is to be kept as a model of values to which we aspire as a nation. The only worthy Jefferson must also be finite. Yet the Jefferson that has seized the American historical imagination is the Jefferson of nearly infinite wisdom on questions of freedom.

His baffling complexity on all other matters has been the subject of critical analysis from his own time to the present. Historians have been fascinated with him as a figure of contradictions and ambiguities. The incandescent advocate of natural rights was a slaveholder; the strict constructionist of constitutional powers purchased Louisiana and adopted the embargo; the philosopher wrote the *Manual of Parliamentary Practice;* the aristocrat championed democracy; and the democrat never introduced a proposal for universal manhood suffrage. A chiaroscuro of Jefferson would fill a huge canvas. But one image has remained pure and undisputed, if not indisputable: Jefferson the apostle of freedom.

The consensus of historians, particularly of our own time, is made abundantly clear: "Into whatever remote niches the historians pursue Jefferson, they help to illuminate the American faith in freedom. Of freedom, Jefferson speaks to the present with the same urgency as to his own time, and with a voice as affirmative as it is authentic."[30] Occasional inconsistencies between Jefferson's actions and libertarian values have been regarded as momentary aberrations, the exceptions proving the rule. Even unsympathetic historians have endorsed the traditional image. Some have underscored his occasional aberrations, but whether they have done so with the biting irony of Henry Adams or the bitter *tu quoque* of Albert Beveridge, they have never suggested more than the possibility that the democratic idol had a toe of clay.

It is striking that despite the vicissitudes of Jefferson's reputation and the unending controversy on his significance, a Federalist historian has described the Jefferson image that has engendered nearly universal concurrence.

There remains, wrote Richard Hildreth, an undeniable fact about Jefferson, despite his defects of character and statesmanship:

> He was—rarity, indeed, among men of affairs—rarity, indeed, among professed democratical leaders—a sincere and enthusiastic believer in the rights of humanity. And, as in so many other like cases, this faith on his part will ever suffice to cover, as with the mantle of charity, a multitude of sins; nor will there ever be wanting a host of worshipers—living ideas being of vastly more consequence to posterity than dead actions passed and gone—to mythicize him into a political saint . . . exalted, by a passionate imagination, far above the heads of contemporary men, who, if they labored, suffered, and accomplished more for that generation, yet loved and trusted universal humanity less.[31]

Claude Bowers and Vernon Parrington, more recently Henry S. Commager, Dumas Malone, Julian Boyd, and Merrill Peterson, have fortified the image that lays claim to our devotion and admiration. Malone's biography of Jefferson, for example, opens with the theme: "Liberty was his chief concern, and his major emphasis was on the freedom of the spirit and the mind."[32] Boyd, praising Peterson's book, expressed pleasure that "in these pages the image of Jefferson that finally emerges is that of a figure of universal dimensions, wholly committed to the rights of man."[33] However, the Jefferson theme has scarcely been exhausted, because the informed scholar now realizes "how little is *really* known about Jefferson . . . Jefferson is an old, old subject: but the quest for the historical Jefferson, under the formal discipline of scholarly inquiry, is young."[34] If the historical Jefferson is the Jefferson *of his time,* a shadow may fall over the image of the apostle of freedom, for he had a darker side.

Freedom's apostle was not its apostate. Yet Jefferson's thoughts and actions on a variety of occasions and issues over an extended period followed a pattern that does not easily square with the conventional image. The purpose here is to sketch that pattern and to seek an understanding of it. If the focus is upon the darker side only, the reason is that the other Jefferson, the familiar one of the conventional image, is too well known to require depiction. It is the unfamiliar Jefferson who needs to be studied, the Jefferson who wrote the following letter shortly after the acquittal of Burr and his fellow conspirators:

> I did wish to see these people get what they deserved; and under the maxim of the law itself, that *inter arma silent leges,* that in an encampment expecting daily attack from a powerful enemy, self-preservation is paramount to all law, I expected that instead of invoking the forms of the law to cover traitors, all good citizens would have concurred in securing them. Should we have ever gained our Revolution, if we had bound our hands by manacles of the law, not only in the beginning, but in any part of the revolutionary conflict? There are extreme cases where the laws become inadequate even to their own preservation, and where the universal resource is a dictator, or martial law.[35]

The unfamiliar Jefferson at one time or another supported loyalty oaths; countenanced internment camps for political suspects; drafted a bill of attainder; urged prosecutions for seditious libel; trampled on the Fourth Amendment; condoned military despotism; used the Army to enforce laws in time of peace; censored reading; chose professors for their political opinions; and endorsed the doctrine that the means, however odious, were justified by the ends.

The conventional image of Jefferson was partially

fashioned from a national impulse to have a libertarian hero larger than life. When the American people honor Jefferson as freedom's foremost exponent, they reflect their own ideals and aspirations more, perhaps, than they reflect history. The darker side of both Jefferson and of the American experience is not venerated, but its existence is undeniable. American history yields more than one tradition. Abridgments of civil liberty are as old a story as the nation itself; Jefferson embodied and reflected both traditions.

Much of his reputation and even his influence derived from his habitual repetition of inspired reveries about freedom, expressed in memorable aphorisms. On countless occasions, for example, he testified to his belief in liberty of the press; his maxims on the subject earned him a place with Milton and Mill. However, there were significant inconsistencies between his deeds and his words. He experimented with censorship and condoned the prosecution of his critics. In the long run his pen was mightier than his practice, for his rhetoric helped to create an American creed and to shape the standards by which even he must be measured.

He must be measured only by the standards of his own time. More often than not they were his own, by adoption rather than by invention. With rare exception he fastened, almost as if by instinct, upon the best and broadest in a great heritage of English liberty. He and his generation were the heirs to a legacy from Milton, Locke, Sydney, and, even more importantly, from Coke and the seventeenth century common lawyers. Writs protecting the "liberty of the subject" as well as the "natural rights of man" defined the guarantees of personal freedom that found expression in most American bills of rights. Virginia's, for example, embodied in constitutional form common-law rights traceable to a history antedating Magna Carta, extending through the Habeas Corpus Act and the English Bill of Rights, rights long given customary expression in Virginia courts. Virginia sometimes improved upon and extended British practice. Although the innovations were few, they were of genuine importance as in the case of separation of church and state or in the careful definition of treason, in both of which Jefferson played a dominating role. By the time he became president, the many clauses of the federal and various state bills of rights testified to a widespread understanding of civil libertarian principles. Observance of them varied from state to state, but not because they were unknown. On the contrary, during Jefferson's lifetime, there was never an issue for which incontestably familiar libertarian standards were lacking to guide his judgment. Experience with the application of certain of those standards may have been slim. Yet the standards themselves had been established.

Jefferson could not possibly have lived up to history's depictions and expectations—for no man could have—but his performance may be reasonably measured by the best practices of his time. His lapses, which were abundant, did not result from hypocrisy or meanness of spirit. His darker side derived, rather, in some instances from the fact that he was simply not as libertarian as later Americans liked to believe; in others, from the fact that circumstances seemed to him to require a course that sacrificed libertarian considerations for even larger ends. He held public office for over a third of a century and continued a lively involvement in public affairs for long after. Almost always at or near the center of power, where both political expediency and official responsibility tempered ideological commitment, he sometimes found it easy to believe that libertarian claims were outweighed in importance by competing interests.

Jefferson's record on religious liberty was really quite exceptional—an almost consistent demonstration of devotion to principle. He was even more devoted to free or popular government, and his fears for its safety accounted, however paradoxically, for his unlibertarian behavior. Intensely nationalistic, he believed that God had singled out the United States to demonstrate to all the world that without privileged orders—without monarchy, aristocracy, or church—the rational ideals of the Enlightenment could become daily realities in the lives of all men. His was a messianic nationalism, founded on principles of political freedom as expressed in the Declaration of Independence. "We feel," he wrote during his first administration, "that we are acting under obligations not confined to the limits of our own society. It is impossible not to be sensible that we are acting for all mankind; that circumstances denied to others, but indulged to us, have imposed on us the duty of proving what is the degree of freedom and self-government in which a society may venture to leave its individual members."[36] "The station which we occupy among the nations of the earth," he declared on the day he left the presidency, "is honorable, but awful. Trusted with the destinies of this solitary republic of the world, the only monument of human rights, and the sole depository of the sacred fire of freedom and self-government, from hence it is to be lighted up in other regions of the earth, if other regions of the earth shall ever become susceptible of its benign influence. All mankind ought then, with us, to rejoice in its prosperous, and sympathize in its adverse fortunes, as involving everything dear to man."[37] In 1820 he wrote: "We exist . . . as standing proofs that a government, so modelled as to rest continually on the will of the whole society, is a practicable government."[38]

The enemies of the Republic both at home and abroad, Jefferson believed, longed for its destruction. To prevent that required strong, decisive measures, even at the risk of temporarily abridging civil liberties. A government too weak to establish and protect itself could scarcely bequeath the sacred chalice of freedom to the next generation. In Jefferson's eyes, the Republic was in nearly constant peril from the time of its birth. It would have been stillborn if the British and their Tory allies had had their way. It would have been cut down in its infancy had their successors, the ultra-Federalists, prevailed at the turn of the century. It would have withered and died if the disunionist activities of the Essex Junto had triumphed from the time of the purchase of Louisiana through the War of 1812; or if Aaron Burr had succeeded in his conspiracy to sever the West. It would have had the dimmest future if the centralized Leviathan of Hamilton, Marshall, and John Quincy Adams had stifled the local roots of democracy. It would have been thwarted and throttled if the aggressions of Britain and Bonaparte had been submitted to or had involved the United States in an untimely war. In short, Jefferson believed that the nation lived in a continual crisis, the security of its republican institutions menaced internally and by foreign foes.

Although he exaggerated, the dangers were real enough, increasing the natural difficulties attending the American experiment with freedom. Men did not then take for granted that the new nation would survive. History and the opinions of celebrated political theorists predicted failure. The federal system was still a novelty and had not yet proved itself. No other republic in history had dared to govern so extensive a territory, and no nation had begun its political existence without first achieving a cultural nationalism. The extraordinary diversity of the United States was commonly regarded as a handicap: it was composed of too many governments, local traditions, races, languages, religions, national stocks, and economic interests to survive as a unity. In the face of so many centrifugal forces, there was no king, no national church, no army, and few centripetal loyalties to provide unity. Unique political forms only seemed to compound the problem. The situation of the new nation would not inspire confidence in its future if the principles of the Revolution, which Jefferson believed to be its major asset and cement, were corrupted or betrayed.

The economic policies of the Federalists during the 1790's gave him reason to fear such corruption. The Alien and Sedition Acts hardened his opinion. In the crisis of 1798–1800, the Federalists threatened to abort the development of freedom in the United States. Deterioration of relations with France had created the opportunity and cover for a thrust for power by a highly placed political elite with little faith in the capacity of the people for self-government. These men, who composed the ultra-Federalist faction, conceived of themselves as an aristocracy not of land and bloodline but of political virtue and fitness to rule—rule rather than govern. Impatient with political compromise and incapable of distinguishing dissent from disloyalty, they were prepared to use legal and military coercion to control public opinion for party purposes. They were prepared, too, to abandon a foreign policy of neutrality and nonintervention in exchange for foreign intrigues and military conquest. Even war was planned as an instrument of party policy. Distrustful of free elections, they were intolerant of freedom of the press and of free political opposition. Their efforts to institutionalize vigilantism and repression were noxiously at variance with the elementary Jeffersonian principles of a republican society.

Although they were defeated in 1800, largely as a result of the rupture within their own party, Jefferson never abandoned a total distrust of their leaders and always suspected the worst from them. Throughout the Napoleonic period, when Bonapartism stood as a constant and disillusioning reminder that a liberal revolution could be destroyed from within, and when a constant crisis in foreign affairs acutely jeopardized the peaceable development of the United States, Jefferson detected the telltale signs that warned of betrayal. Secessionist plots in the Northeast and dismemberment plots in the West; civil disobedience along the Atlantic coast during the embargo era; assaults on the Constitution from the federal judiciary; unbelievably ferocious libels from the opposition press—all these and more had the depressing tendency of requiring from him uncongenial countermeasures, often unlibertarian, to save the experiment in liberty from its enemies. The paradox was apparent. Equally so was the muting of his principles and the pattern of inconsistency in their application.

✧ Chapter Two ✧

In Times That Tried Men's Souls: The American Revolution

JEFFERSON's conduct during the Revolutionary War often conformed with the maxim *inter arma silent leges* (in time of war the laws are silent). The benefits of another maxim, more congenial to the spirit of liberty, *fiat justitia ruat coelum* (let justice be done though heaven fall), were denied to citizens suspected of Tory thoughts and sympathies.

A long hard war was scarcely a propitious time for respecting, let alone nurturing, civil liberties. The imperatives of victory and political survival superseded the moral values that normally claimed the devotion of humane, libertarian leaders. During the Revolution Jefferson, like Washington, the Adamses, and Paine, believed that there could be no toleration for serious differences of political opinion on the issue of independence, no acceptable alternative to complete submission to the patriot cause. Everywhere there was unlimited liberty to praise it, none to criticize it. Freedom of speech attached only to the speech of liberty. The Continental Congress, early in 1776, urged the states to enact legislation to prevent the people from being "deceived and drawn into erroneous opinion."[1]

Jefferson, as a member of Congress, a leader of the Virginia legislature, and a wartime governor, was an enemy of erroneous opinion.

He and John Adams were a committee of the Congress that drafted the Continental Articles and Rules for the Better Government of the Troops.[2] These first American articles of war, adopted in 1776, emulated a British model that punished by court-martial any "traitorous or disrespectful words" against the king or members of the royal family. Instead of eliminating the provision altogether, Adams and Jefferson retained the restraint on freedom of speech by making criminal the use of "traitorous or disrespectful words" against the authority of the United States or the legislature of any state in which the offender might be quartered.[3] This measure remained in effect until 1806, when Jefferson was President.

In 1804 one of Jefferson's strongest supporters in Congress, Representative Joseph Varnum of Massachusetts, urged wholesale revision of the Articles of War because the code adopted in 1776 had become outdated in many respects. Varnum asked that the protection against traitorous and disrespectful speech include the president and vice-president, as well as Congress.[4] Representative Joseph Nicholson of Maryland, an equally staunch Jeffersonian, denounced the provision as placing a "fence round the President, Vice-President, and Congress, with a second sedition law."[5] He questioned the constitutionality of the vague crime of "traitorous words," presumably unaware that the clause was the handiwork of a committee that had included President Jefferson. Nicholson's objections delayed House action until 1806, when the Articles of War were revised. Article Five of the new code substituted for "traitorous" the less obnoxious but more comprehensive term "contemptuous." Any officer or soldier in peacetime or wartime using "contemptuous or disrespectful words" against the president, vice president, or Congress might be punished by court-martial.[6] A member of the Judge Advocate General's Corps has observed:

> Plainly, the right to use 'contemptuous or disrespectful words' against the President, the Vice-President, Congress, and state governors or legislatures is of the essence of the civil liberties of a citizen; such language thus directed is indeed a matter of daily occurrence; and when the Sedition Act of 1798 impinged on such activity, it was a matter of abiding conviction on the part of Jefferson and his followers that this measure was unconstitutional in the face of the first amendment's command that Congress shall not make any law 'abridging the freedom of speech.' But no Jeffersonian in Congress objected once the word 'traitorous' was stricken, and Jefferson himself signed the bill that enacted article 5 of 1806 into law.[7]

President Jefferson was not even slightly disturbed by the obnoxious restraint imposed on the freedom of speech of soldiers. The fact that he and others identified with civil liberty were originally responsible for the code of 1776 and its subsequent extension has been used to support the constitutionality of present military regulations imposing conformity, discipline, and subordination, such as Article Eighty-Eight of the present Uniform Code of Military Justice, restricting the speech of members of the armed forces.[8] A case can be made against the enjoyment by the military of the same scope of free speech as civilians. But it is well to remember that the fundamental liberty of speech

> stands as an end in itself, deserving our defense against every encroachment not required by some competing in-

terest critical to our survival. A person who enters the armed services remains an individual, a possessor of rights as well as a subject of duties, and his sacrifices of basic liberties should be kept to a minimum. A government which boasts that it is a government of, for, and by the people—all the people—cannot reduce millions of men to second class citizens.[9]

That observation applies with even greater force to Jefferson's lifetime, when the backbone of the army, as he himself insisted, was the people's militia and when pressures for conformity and direct dangers to national security were comparatively rare. The code of 1776 was a product of war and copied from British precedent; but the extension of that code in time of peace, under a Constitution protecting freedom of speech, and after the experience of the Sedition Act, indicated a certain insensitivity to the values of the First Amendment.

During the Revolution, the civilian counterpart of the provision in the military code on traitorous opinions was embodied in two related measures passed by the Virginia legislature while Jefferson was its chief draftsman. One was an act against "crimes injurious to the Independence of America, but less than treason"; the other was a loyalty oath. Jefferson certainly supported both and probably had a hand in writing the former which was a companion piece to an act against treason that he did write.[10] His treason statute of 1776, a vast improvement over British models, carefully defined the crime as levying war against the commonwealth, adhering to its enemies and giving them aid and comfort; the statute also required two voluntary witnesses to prove the "open deed."[11]

The act against crimes less than treason, however, was

in part a loosely drawn interdict against freedom of political expression. It may, of course, be legitimate and even necessary in time of war to punish seditious conduct, such as obstructing the execution of war measures, and even to proscribe direct and immediate incitements to seditious conduct, such as exciting resistance to the government. But the line between defensible war measures and deliberate repression of "erroneous" opinion has been passed when the crime is also defined as "any word," or attempt to "persuade," in behalf of the authority of the king or parliament. For these traitorous but not treasonable words and activities, the statute fixed a maximum sentence of five years' imprisonment and a fine of £20,000.[12] The statute also commanded that it be publicly read by the sheriff of every county and the minister of every church, on pain of a ten-pound fine "to be recovered with costs by the informer before the court of the county."

The legislature revised and expanded this statute, in 1780, to include new verbal crimes "inferior in malignity to treason" but injurious to independence. A maximum fine of one hundred thousand pounds' weight of crop tobacco and five years' imprisonment was the punishment for any person who "by writing, or by printing, or by open preaching, or by express words" should maintain that the United States or any part of it was dependent upon the British crown or parliament, or should acknowledge the king to be sovereign or himself a subject of the king, or should attribute to Great Britain any authority over the United States, or should wish health, prosperity, or success to the king, or should induce anyone to express any of the prohibited sentiments. Governor Jefferson signed the bill into law.[13]

The actual enforcement of the act was tempered by a spirit of forgiveness, since persons imprisoned for their criminal opinions were offered pardons if they would take the oath of loyalty to the Commonwealth.[14] The statute was a useful dragnet against persons who could not be convicted for the greater crime of treason. Jefferson, for example, ordered the imprisonment of all persons in besieged Gloucester and York counties against whom "legal evidence cannot be obtained" despite "Suspicion that they have been guilty of the offences of treason or Misprision of Treason, or . . . are disaffected to the Independence of the United States, and will, when Occasion serves, aid or advise the Operations of the Enemy." Persons imprisoned on mere suspicion that they had or *might* aid the enemy during military emergency awaited the governor's pleasure on the disposition of their cases.[15]

The loyalty oath, passed at the May 1777 session of the legislature, was an unreasoned effort to enforce true patriotism despite the claims of conscience. The chief purposes of the oath were to coerce loyalty and to identify for purposes of punishment every person who, in Jefferson's phrase, was "a traitor in thought, but not in deed."[16] The punishment was severe. Nonjurors were stripped of their civil rights, although forced to pay additional taxes. They were also subjected to public opprobrium and to possible internment. Jefferson and Washington agreed that only those who swore loyalty to American Independence should enjoy the rights of citizenship and that all others were "secret enemies."[17] All states by 1778 had adopted loyalty or test oaths, "weapons of savage coercion" that failed to distinguish between loyalty itself and the ritual of swearing it.[18]

The Virginia statute required all free males above the age of sixteen to renounce the British crown and swear allegiance to Virginia "as a free and independent state," and to inform on "all treasons or traitorous conspiracies which . . . now or hereafter shall . . . be formed against this or any of the United States of America." Nonjurors were disarmed and lost all rights to vote, hold public office, serve on juries, sue for debts, or buy property.[19] By a supplementary act of the next session, nonjurors were also subject to double taxation.[20] Jefferson had a hand in drafting a statute in 1778 by which triple taxation was inflicted on all nonjurors or recusants.[21] He also drafted a revised form of the oath for "every person, by law required to give assurance of fidelity," but did not alter its substance.[22]

Jefferson also supported a statute which legalized the Age of Enlightenment's rudimentary precursor of modern internment camps for political suspects. The statute had its origin in a war measure of the state's Committee of Safety. On April 10, 1776, the Committee of Safety ordered all persons in Norfolk and Princess Anne counties who supported Lord Dunmore to move into the interior at least thirty miles from the enemy. This measure, however ruthless, was justified by the military necessity of cutting Dunmore off from provisions and intelligence supplied by local Tories; it applied to those who had taken Dunmore's oath of allegiance to the British crown.[23]

Strong medicine became stronger still when the Governor's Council in August 1777 ordered militia commanders to remove beyond military zones and to restrain all persons who refused to take the oath of loyalty to the American cause or who were merely suspected of disaffection. The order "affected a good many people, and the assembly, at its meeting in the fall, fearing that the executive had acted unconstitutionally, passed a special act of immunity."[24] The immunity statute, framed by a committee of which Jefferson was a member, "indemnified" and "exonerated" the governor and members of his council from any suits brought by or on behalf of any persons who had been evacuated and interned.[25] Jefferson thus participated in retroactively constitutionalizing the executive act by which political suspects and nonjurors were interned because they *might* commit a crime at some future time.

The only extenuation of the act was that it was occasioned by the "appearance of a hostile Fleet in the Bay of the Chesapeake," sought to prevent the communication of military intelligence, and was limited in operation to "the Imminence of the Danger." When the expected invasion did not materialize, Tory sympathizers were allowed to return to their homes. But three years later, when an invasion was anticipated, Governor Jefferson, who was known for his scrupulous constitutional conscience, was vested by the legislature with "extraordinary powers." One provision of the statute declared:

> That the governor be authorized, with advice of council . . . to commit to close confinement, any person or persons whatsoever, whom there may be just cause to suspect of disaffection to the independence of the United States, and of attachment to their enemies; or to cause any such persons to be removed to such places of security as may best guard against the effects of their influence and arts to injure this community, and benefit the common enemy.[26]

It does not appear that Jefferson, who signed the bill, ever ordered the internment of any part of the population in "places of security," possibly because he failed to sense the danger of an invasion,[27] or because he could not afford to withdraw militia from field duty to serve as guards.[28] But Jefferson did exercise his power to imprison the disaffected or politically suspect, and many languished in jail without a hearing or even a court-martial. In one case, twenty-five Tories in the Henrico jail complained to the governor that they had been confined for six months without trial, and asked for an examination before any court or release on bail pending examination. In another case, a man protested that he had been under military arrest for sixteen days without being able to secure a copy of the charges against him.[29]

The most striking departure from standards of due process of law was undoubtedly the bill of attainder and outlawry, drafted by Jefferson, against Josiah Philips and unnamed members of his gang of robbers. No instrument of criminal jurisprudence was more dreaded or violative of fair procedures than a bill of attainder and outlawry. The bloody history of such bills gained in infamy because of their use as weapons of political vengeance in Stuart England. Parliament, whether Puritan or Royalist, had discovered that the most expeditious way of condemning a political opponent was to pronounce his guilt and sentence him to death, thereby bypassing the niceties of the common-law courts, or the necessity on the part of the Commons to secure from the Lords a conviction for impeachment.[30]

Outlawry was in bad odor in England as far back as 1215 when the celebrated thirty-ninth chapter of the Magna Carta provided that "No freeman shall be taken or imprisoned or disseised, or outlawed, or exiled, or anyways destroyed . . . unless by the lawful judgment of his peers, or by the law of the land." One could still be declared outside the protection of the law and be treated as a wild beast whom any man might slay with impunity; but an elaborate common-law procedure, involving the courts and county coroners, insured some standard of fairness in the declaration of outlawry.

In the celebrated case of John Wilkes who was convicted in absentia for criminal libels and then outlawed when he failed to appear for sentence, Lord Chief Justice Mansfield in 1770 reversed the sentence for outlawry, which even he found repugnant, by grasping at the most trivial technicalities.[31] Wilkes was a symbol of liberty to revolutionary America, his prosecution in every respect held up as a symbol of tyranny. It almost passes belief that Jefferson and his associates could have engaged in an outlawry—and one which bypassed common-law procedures. It does pass belief that Jefferson many years later, and after the United States Constitution prohibited bills of attainder by the states or national government, defended the abhorrent act of 1778.

Josiah Philips was reputed to be a Tory cutthroat who used a British commission as a shield for plundering and terrorizing the countryside. On May 1, 1778, the Council received word that Philips, "the noted Traitor has again made an insurrection in Princess Anne County at the head of fifty Men." At the Council's authorization, Governor Patrick Henry called out twice that number of militiamen and offered a reward of $500 for the capture of Philips, dead or alive. But by the end of the month word arrived from the local commander that the "cowardly" militia having failed miserably in locating the desperadoes, the only hope lay in flushing them from "their secret places in the swamp" by removing their relations and friends from the vicinity. Henry placed the matter before the assembly.[32] He also consulted Thomas Jefferson, then its influential member, who later recalled, "We both thought the best proceeding would be by bill of attainder, unless he [Philips] delivered himself up for trial within a given time."[33]

The assembly, without debate, promptly adopted a bill of attainder, written by Jefferson, that convicted Josiah Philips for having levied war against the commonwealth, committed murder, burned houses, and wasted farms. The bill alleged that "the usual forms and procedures of the courts of law" would leave the people exposed to further crimes, and provided that if Philips and his confederates did not surrender to some lawful authority within one month, they "shall stand and be convicted and attainted of high treason, and shall suffer the pains of death, and incur all forfeitures [of all property] . . . And that the good people of this commonwealth may not in the meantime be subject to the unrestrained hostilities of the said insurgents, *Be it farther enacted,* That from and after the passing of this act it shall be lawful for any person, with or without orders, to pursue and slay the said Josiah Philips, and any others who have been of his associates."[34] Perhaps the most sinister aspect of the bill was its declaration of an open hunting season on the unnamed men whose guilt for treason and murder was legislatively assumed. Any of Philips' "associates" might be killed on the mere supposition that he shared his leader's guilt; a man might be shot on the mere supposition that he was an "associate" of Philips.

Within the month Philips and several of his followers were captured after a battle in which one of his men was killed. Since the bill of attainder had not yet by law become operative, the prisoners were regularly indicted and tried. But the crime charged against them was not high treason, not even murder or arson; it was only robbery of twenty-eight men's felt hats and five pounds of twine, valued at forty-five shillings! Robbery, however, was a capital felony, so that the convicted men were executed.[35]

Jefferson later explained that Edmund Randolph, then the attorney general of Virginia, pressed only the robbery charge in the expectation that Philips would plead that he was a British subject taken in arms, under a commission from Lord Dunmore, in support of his sovereign and was therefore a prisoner of war entitled to the protection of the law of nations.[36] Philips, as a matter of fact, did make this plea. It was rejected by the court on the ground that a citizen's crimes cannot be justified by a commission from the enemy. The court might have handed down the same ruling with equal facility had the charge been high treason or any of the capital felonies specified in the act of the legislature. That only a charge of robbery was pressed suggested that the evidence of treason and murder would not stand up in court, making the legislature's assumption of his guilt rather arbitrary, as well as grossly violative of Article Eight of the Virginia Declaration of Rights which had been adopted only two years earlier.[37] Worse still for the reputations of the legislature and Jefferson, men closely associated with the case, including Randolph and Henry, quickly forgot that the criminals, despite the attainder, had been executed after receiving due process of law.[38] What was remembered was the abhorrent and undeniable fact that Virginia had employed a bill of attainder.

In 1788, for example, when the Virginia ratifying convention debated the proposed national constitution, Randolph was irked beyond endurance by Henry's demagogic complaint that liberty was being sacrificed in the absence of a bill of rights. Rising to declare that parchment guarantees were no insurance against legislative violation, Randolph reminded the convention:

> There is one example of this violation in Virginia, of a most striking and shocking nature—an example so horrid, that, if I conceived my country would passively permit a repetition of it, dear as it is to me, I would seek means of expatriating myself from it. A man, who was then a citizen, was deprived of his life thus: from a mere reliance on general reports, a gentleman in the House of Delegates informed the house that a certain man [Josiah Philips] had committed several crimes, and was running at large, perpetrating other crimes. He therefore moved for leave to attaint him . . . he was attainted very speedily and precipitately, without any proof better than vague reports. Without being confronted with his accusers and witnesses, without the privilege of calling for evidence in his behalf, he was sentenced to death, and was afterwards actually executed . . . I cannot contemplate it without horror.[39]

Randolph later added that Philips "had a commission in his pocket at that time. He was, therefore, only a prisoner of war."[40]

Randolph had given the impression that the execution was the result of the bill of attainder; Henry amazingly endorsed the misinformation as fact. Philips, he argued, had been no Socrates. "He was a fugitive murderer and an outlaw . . . Those who declare war against the human race may be struck out of existence as soon as they are apprehended. He was not executed according to those beautiful legal ceremonies which are pointed out by the laws in criminal cases. The enormity of his crimes did not entitle him to it."[41]

Of the several rejoinders to this defense of the bill of attainder, John Marshall's was the most incisive:

> Can we pretend to the enjoyment of political freedom or security, when we are told that a man has been, by an act of Assembly, struck out of existence without a trial by jury, without examination, without being confronted with his accusers and witnesses, without the benefits of the law of the land? Where is our safety, when we are told that this act was justifiable because the person was not a Socrates? What has become of the worthy member's maxims? Is this one of them? Shall it be a maxim that a man shall be deprived of his life without the benefit of law? Shall such a deprivation of life be justified by answering, that the man's life was not taken *secundum artem* because he was a bad man?[42]

These remarks demonstrate the profound repugnance with which a bill of attainder was regarded by fair-minded men and provide a standard by which to measure Jefferson's subsequent defense of his handiwork.

In 1815, thirty-seven years after the event, when he received the proof sheets of Girardin's continuation of Burk's *History of Virginia,* Jefferson commented at length on the Philips case. Objecting to the quotations from the Virginia debates and from St. George Tucker's edition of Blackstone, he recommended that "the whole of the quotations from Tucker, Randolph and Henry, be struck out" and that his own version of the case, running to two pages, be inserted in their place. Tucker was criticized for having written a "diatribe" against bills of attainder, instead of having defined their "occasion and proper office."

Legislative outlawry and attainder was justifiable, Jefferson argued, when a person charged with crime withdrew from justice or forcibly resisted it. In such a case the legislature should give him sufficient time to appear for trial and declare that his refusal be taken as a confession of guilt. Bills of attainder, Jefferson acknowledged, had been abused in England, but "what institution is insusceptible of abuse in wicked hands?" As for Philips, he had been tried by common law, although he had "not come in before the day prescribed." Indeed, had Philips been denied jury trial, confrontation, and the right to produce evidence in his own behalf, "I would have asked of the Attorney General," he claimed, "why he proposed or permitted it."[43] This inconsistent comment revealed that Jefferson was on the defensive and raised the question of why the bill of attainder had been needed at all if common-law process were to have been followed despite it. In such a case, an indictment would have served to charge the defendant. But an indictment, of course, did not perform the function of a bill of attainder: declaring the guilt and fixing the punishment of the accused without court and common-law process.

Jefferson, despite the inconsistent lapse, had not at all changed his opinion. Continuing his attack on Randolph, he declared that if the former attorney general had meant that Philips had been denied constitutionally guaranteed procedures on the passage of the attainder, "how idle to charge the legislature with omitting to confront the culprit with his witnesses, when he was standing out in arms and in defiance of their authority." The observation was sophistical, since it would have been even more idle to have expected the culprit to surrender when his guilt had already been explicitly determined and announced by the legislature. That body had also declared that "the usual forms and procedures of the courts of law," being insufficient, would not be followed. Jefferson's position was baldly exposed when he added:

> No one pretended then that the perpetrator of crimes who could successfully resist the officers of justice, should be protected in the continuance of them by the privileges of his citizenship, and that baffling ordinary process, nothing extraordinary could be rightfully adopted to protect the citizens against him. No one doubted that society had a right to erase from the roll of its members any one who rendered his own existence inconsistent with theirs; to withdraw from him the protection of their laws, and to remove him from among them by exile, or even by death if necessary.[44]

In forwarding to Patrick Henry's apologetic biographer a copy of this lengthy letter to Girardin, Jefferson concluded: "I was then [1778] thoroughly persuaded of the correctness of the proceeding, and am more and more convinced by reflection. If I am in error, it is an error of principle. I know of no substitute for the process of outlawry, so familiar to our law, or to it's [*sic*] kindred process by act of attainder, duly applied, which could have reached the case of Josiah Philips."[45] Thus, Jefferson in the end agreed fundamentally with Patrick Henry's statement in 1788, notwithstanding John Marshall's answer. On careful reflection, by 1815, Jefferson still strongly endorsed outlawry and a bill of attainder.

His position was all the more surprising because Jefferson himself, in 1783, had proposed a new constitution for Virginia which explicitly denied to the legislature any power "to pass any bill of attainder, (or other law declaring any person guilty) of treason or felony."[46]

✧ Chapter Three ✧

A Few Wholesome Prosecutions: The Problem of a Free Press

JEFFERSON's initial attempt at constitution-making was in 1776.[1] His draft of a state constitution, which was received too late in Williamsburg to be of much influence, reflected carelessness or indifference about civil liberties. To be sure, he salted his proposed constitution with guarantees of certain rights. But the task was done with neither the care, the passion, nor the eloquence that characterized George Mason's work. Jefferson knew that the Virginia convention intended to frame a Declaration of Rights, yet he did not include one in his draft. The omission is particularly striking when compared to the superb declaration drafted chiefly by Mason and adopted by the convention. Mason's declaration protected many rights, some in detail and always in elegant language; Jefferson, by contrast, protected few rights and in terse, matter-of-fact language. Mason began philosophically with an epitome of the theory of natural rights and popular government. Jefferson was not only less the philosopher; he was less the lawyer, for he omitted guarantees against exclusive privileges, excessive bail, general search warrants, compulsory self-incrimination, and most of the positive rights of the criminally accused which Mason enumerated. On the other hand, Jefferson would have granted a fifty-acre freehold to every propertyless male citizen and proposed too that no person "hereafter" could be held in slavery.

Jefferson's proposal on religious liberty would have separated church and state, thereby anticipating the great Bill for Establishing Religious Freedom, drawn by him in 1779 and adopted in 1786. But the first two drafts of his 1776 religious-liberty clause suggest the narrowness of his thinking on the scope of *political* expression. The first draft, after declaring that no person should be compelled to frequent or maintain any religious service or institution, added, "but seditious behavior to be punble by civil magistrate accdg to the laws already made or hereafter to be made."[2] On reconsideration he bracketed but did not red pencil the words quoted. In his second draft, the impulse to punish politically unacceptable opinions was again expressed in the following clause: "but this [the liberty of religious opinions] shall not be held to justify any seditious preaching or conversation against the authority of the civil government."[3] Again on reconsideration, Jefferson bracketed the quoted words. He was apparently groping for a way to insure the unfettered right to propagate religious opinions without relinquishing the power of the state to curb dangerous political expressions and without permitting freedom for seditious opinions under the guise of religious expression.

In the end Jefferson omitted the restrictive clause

from the third and final draft, possibly because he recognized that the task at hand was to insure religious liberty rather than to acknowledge the unquestioned power of the state to prosecute seditious libels. The right to religious liberty, moreover, was the one above all others to which he was most deeply devoted, and he was willing to take risks to insure it. His Bill for Establishing Religious Freedom resolved his conflict by adopting the formula, suggested by the Reverend Philip Furneaux, that religious principles should not be the concern of the civil government until they "break out into overt acts against peace and good order."[4]

Significantly, Jefferson never applied the overt-acts test to political, as well as religious, opinions. Although his own faith was deeply held, he was quite indifferent about that of others. In his *Notes on the State of Virginia,* which he began in 1780, he remarked that whether his neighbor said that there were twenty gods or none "neither picks my pocket nor breaks my leg."[5] But political opinions could pick his pocket or break his leg: he worried about permitting religiously founded opinions "against the civil government"; he supported political test oaths; he denied civil rights to nonjurors; and he was ready to imprison carriers of "traitorous opinions" in time of crisis.

His threshold of tolerance for hateful political ideas was less than generous. Eloquently and felicitously he declared himself in favor of freedom of speech and press, but invariably either in favor of the liberty of his own political allies or merely in abstract propositions. Under concrete circumstances he found it easy to make exceptions when the freedom of his enemies was at stake.

The question is not whether Jefferson favored freedom of political opinion, but how far he would go in its support. The vaguely defined principle of liberty of expression had no opponents in Jefferson's America. Only seditious libels, licentious opinions, and malicious falsehoods were condemned. The determining factor was the meaning given these terms when one's own principles were the speaker's target. Freedom to denounce the rocks and rills was scarcely an issue, nor even freedom to shout seditious opinions from a lonely mountain top. The test of free speech, or press, was whether a man could with impunity express himself openly to his fellow citizens even in times of stress and on matters that counted deeply. Freedom for the other fellow was the test, not freedom for the friendly opponent but for the one with the detested and outrageous opinions who challenged on fundamentals and whose criticism cut to the bone. Jefferson simply did not concern himself about such freedom. He cared deeply for the intellectual liberty of religious, scientific, or philosophical heretics, but not for the freedom of opinion of political heretics —unless political heresies of his own adherence were involved.

Jeremy Bentham in 1776 argued that a free government must permit, indeed partially depended for its existence upon, the freedom with which "malcontents may communicate their sentiments, concert their plans, and practice every mode of opposition short of actual revolt, before the executive power can be legally justified in disturbing them."[6] Frances Maseres insisted that the "dangerous tendency" of allegedly seditious words must be "real and manifest," must, that is, have "actually occasioned the disturbance which [they] seemed to be intended to create."[7] Manasseh Dawes in 1785 declared that sedition can never be committed by mere words, but only by "violent acts."[8]

Jefferson, by contrast, never protested against the substantive law of seditious libel, not even during the Sedition Act controversy. His protests at that time were directed against national as opposed to state prosecution for verbal crimes. He accepted without question the dominant view of his generation that government could be criminally assaulted merely by the expression of critical opinions that allegedly tended to subvert it by lowering it in the public's esteem. His consistent recognition of the concept of verbal political crimes throughout the Revolution continued in the period of peace that followed.

His draft constitution for Virginia in 1783 proposed that the press "shall be subject to no other restraint than liableness to legal prosecution for false facts printed and published."[9] He wrote this as an amendment to the general principle expressed in the Declaration of Rights of 1776, "That the freedom of the press is one of the great bulwarks of liberty, and can never be restrained but by despotic governments."[10] His amendment explicitly opened the door to criminal prosecutions. Yet he framed that amendment after considering the contrary opinion of his neighbors and constituents. In their Albemarle County Instructions concerning the Virginia Constitution, they had recommended an expansion of the freedom guaranteed to the press by the Declaration of Rights. "In regard to the freedom of the press," they urged, "which certainly is, as mentioned in the Bill of Rights, one of the great bulwarks of Liberty, we think that the Printers should never be liable for anything they print, provided they may give up authors, who are responsible, but on the contrary that they should print nothing without."[11] Thus the recommendation from Albemarle favored exempting the press from prosecution for any signed opinions or news. "False facts," or "falsehoods" as Jefferson initially phrased his provision on the press, were singled out for prosecution by him in the face of a more liberal recommendation.

In politics one man's truth is another's falsity. To endorse a state trial for the crime of falsity in political matters was to circumscribe the scope of political expression by the prejudices, or preferences for truth, of the government or the community. By necessary implication, punishment for false facts protected "truthful" statements—whatever they might be in the realm of politics. Jefferson at least would have improved the common law on criminal libels, for the courts assumed that the greater the truth the greater the libel. The legal theory at the time was that the truth of a libel made it even worse because it was more provocative, thereby exacerbating the scandal against the government, its measures, or officials.

Truth as a defense to a charge of libel had been proposed in the celebrated Zenger case in 1735.[12] Jefferson's endorsement of that principle, if indeed his desire to prosecute falsity could be so generously construed, was scarcely daring. For truth as a defense had been the principal contention of *avant-garde* libertarians in England and America throughout the eighteenth century.[13] What was most revealing about Jefferson's proposed provision on the press in 1783 was his failure to challenge the substantive law of criminal libel. He did not even propose that other favorite contention of eighteenth-century libertarians, namely that the jury rather than the judge be empowered to return a verdict on the alleged criminality of a defendant's words.[14]

For all his rhetorical attachment to the abstract principle of a free press, Jefferson distrusted the press; and his distrust soon ripened into choler. Convinced that mendacity was its standard, he once wrote that "our printers ravin on the agonies of their victims, as wolves do on the blood of the lamb."[15] This was his mature view, reflecting a depressing experience with freedom of the press. "It is a melancholy truth," he wrote feelingly, "that a suppression of the press could not more completely deprive the nation of its benefits, than is done by its abandoned prostitution to falsehood. Nothing can now be believed which is seen in a newspaper. Truth itself," he added to this judgment of 1807, "becomes suspicious by being put into that polluted vehicle."[16] His opposition to "falsehood" in the press was a confirmed habit, the result of a thin skin and a strong conviction that the publication of political truth, as he understood it, would lead the people to choose rightly. Prosecution for falsity was a means of inducing the press to inform the public in unobjectionable terms that would leave them free, as he confidently expected, to vote for the party that identified itself with the people.

Jefferson endorsed prosecution again in 1788 when urging Madison to support amendments to the new federal Constitution, including a guarantee for freedom of the press. "A declaration that the federal government will never restrain the presses from printing anything they please, will not take away the liability of the printers for false facts printed. The declaration that religious faith shall be unpunished," he offered as added assurance, "does not give impunity to criminal acts dictated by religious error."[17] Publication of false facts on political matters was apparently the equivalent of an overt crime resulting from a misguided religious conscience. Jefferson's proposal that the press should not be restrained was pure Blackstone. He meant that the press should be free in the English or common-law sense: free from censorship or licensing acts in advance of publication, but responsible for abuse of an unrestrained freedom to publish.[18]

Jefferson received a copy of Madison's proposed amendments to the Constitution in 1789. He was disappointed not to see the adoption of his recommendation on the press. Madison had proposed: "The people shall not be deprived or abridged of their right to speak, to write, or to publish their sentiments; and the freedom of the press, as one of the great bulwarks of liberty, shall be inviolable."[19] Jefferson liked that proposal, he said, but "the following alterations and additions would have pleased me. Art. 4. 'The people shall not be deprived or abridged of their right to speak to write or otherwise to publish anything but false facts affecting injuriously the life, liberty, property, or reputation of others or affecting the peace of the confederacy with foreign nations.' "[20] One can imagine how free the press might have been during the controversies over Jay's Treaty, the Louisiana Purchase, or the embargo, had Jefferson's recommendation prevailed and been taken seriously.

His commitment to fair and open political debate was unquestionable, yet he sometimes did not show it. Witness, for example, the strange letter to Madison in which Jefferson commented on a public meeting in New York City on Jay's Treaty. When Rufus King and Alexander Hamilton tried to speak at the meeting, the mob jammed around the steps of Federal Hall, booed and stamped, and in the end, reported Jefferson, "the Livingstonians appealed to stones & clubs and beat him [Hamilton] & his party off the ground."[21] Whether the report was written "with some glee"[22] is a matter of opinion, but it certainly lacked the censure of mob action that we might have expected from Jefferson.

Jefferson's assault on the Sedition Act of 1798 and his authorship of the Kentucky Resolutions of 1798 and 1799 were not stirring reaffirmations of his faith in a free society. Nowhere is the grand passion of Jefferson's political life supposed to be more apparent than in his opposition to the Federalist "reign of terror."[23] Undoubtedly he believed that he was defending the cause of liberty of political opinion. But his understanding of the cause had not advanced beyond eloquent abstractions, and his position was not as libertarian as has been assumed.

A conviction that the Sedition Act was unconstitutional as well as mortally dangerous to freedom pierced his every thought on the subject. But his thinking was narrow and ritualistic. He intoned "freedom of the press" as if by pronouncing the term he had offered a sovereign remedy. When the occasion called for a fresh analysis of the meaning and scope of free political discussion, he simply expressed abhorrence of the meanness of the Sedition Act's spirit, and reiterated the general proposition that it abridged the First Amendment.

Others, less rigid, but tougher minded, understood that there was a real need for cogently reasoned arguments, indeed for a bold new philosophy. For the Federalists too professed devotion to freedom of the press and the First Amendment. They had a good deal of law and history on their side of the argument on the Sedition Act, and they clothed themselves in the seemingly libertarian garb of Zengerian principles. Indeed, the Sedition Act, despite its partisan enforcement, was an ironic epitome of libertarian thought since the time of Zenger's case, for it embodied all that the libertarians had ever demanded on the subject of freedom of the press. The Sedition Act required that criminal intent be shown; it empowered juries to decide whether the accused's statement was libelous as a matter of law as well as of fact; and it made truth a defense against a charge of criminal libel. Thus the Sedition Act was ostensibly a victory for libertarianism. The victory, however, was instantly recognized as an illusory one, demanding a new definition of the meaning and scope of freedom of political discourse.

Republican spokesmen responded to the challenge, of necessity, with agility and boldness. They constructed a new theory of freedom of speech and press. Wholly abandoning the confining doctrines of Blackstone and the common law, they scornfully denounced the no-prior-restraints definition of liberty.[24] "It would seem a mockery," wrote James Madison, "to say that no laws shall be passed, preventing publications from being made, but that laws might be passed for punishing them in case they should be made."[25] As George Hay put it, the "British definition" meant that a man might be jailed or even put to death for what he published provided that no notice was taken of him before he published.[26]

The new libertarians also rejected the old calculus for measuring the scope of freedom. "Liberty" of the press, for example, had always been differentiated from its "licentiousness," which was the object of the criminal law's sanctions. "Truth" and "facts" had always divided the realm of lawfulness from "falsehoods," and a similar distinction had been made between "good motives" and "malice" or "criminal intent." All such distinctions were now discarded on the ground that they did not distinguish and, therefore, were not meaningful standards that might guide a jury or a court in judging an alleged verbal crime. The terms "licentiousness" or "false," said John Thomson of New York, were "destitute of any meaning," and were used by those who wished "nobody to enjoy the Liberty of the Press but such as were of their own opinion."[27] Punishment of "malice" or intent to defame the government, argued Madison, necessarily struck at the right of free discussion, because critics intended to excite unfavorable sentiments.[28] Finding criminality in the tendency of words was merely an attempt to erect public "tranquility . . . upon the ruins of Civil Liberty," concluded Tunis Wortman in his masterful analysis of freedom.[29]

Wholesale abandonment of the common law's limitations on the press accompanied a withering onslaught against the constrictions and subjectivity of Zengerian principles. The Sedition Act, Hay charged, "appears to be directed against falsehood and malice only; in fact . . . there are many truths, important to society, which are not susceptible of that full, direct, and positive evidence, which alone can be exhibited before a court and a jury."[30] If, argued Albert Gallatin, the Administration prosecuted a citizen for his opinion that the Sedition Act itself was unconstitutional, would not a jury, composed of the friends of that Administration, find the opinion "ungrounded, or, in other words, false and scandalous, and its publication malicious? And by what kind of argument or evidence, in the present temper of parties, could the accused convince them that his opinion was true?"[31] The truth of opinions, the new libertarians contended, could not be proved. Allowing "truth" as a defense and thinking it to be a protection for freedom, Thomson declared, made as much sense as letting a jury decide which was "the most palatable food, agreeable drink, or beautiful color."[32] A jury, he asserted, cannot give an impartial verdict in political trials. The result, agreed Madison, is that the "baleful tendency" of prosecutions for seditious libel "is little diminished by the privilege of giving in evidence the truth of the matter continued in political writings."[33]

The renunciation of traditional concepts reached its climax in the assault on the idea that there was such a crime as seditious libel. The crime, Wortman concluded, could "never be reconciled to the genius and constitution of a Representative Commonwealth."[34] The new libertarianism was genuinely radical because it broke sharply with the past and advocated absolute freedom of political expression. One of its major tenets was that a free government could not be criminally attacked by the opinions of its citizens. Hay, for example, insisted that freedom of the press, like chastity, was either "absolute" or did not exist.[35] Abhorring the very idea of verbal political crimes, he declared that a citizen had a right to "say everything which his passions suggest; he may employ all his time, and all his talents, if he is wicked enough to do so, in speaking against the government matters that are false, scandalous and malicious,"[36] and yet he should be "safe within the sanctuary of the press." He should be safe even if "he censures the measures of our government, and every department and officer thereof, and ascribes the measures of the former, however salutary, and the conduct of the latter, however upright, to the basest motives; even if he ascribes to them measures and acts, which never had existence; thus violating at once, every principle of decency and truth."[37]

In brief the new libertarians advocated that only "injurious conduct," as manifested by "overt acts" or deeds, rather than words, might be criminally redressable.[38] They did not refine this proposition except to recognize that the law of libel should continue to protect private reputations against malicious falsehoods. They would not even recognize that under certain circumstances words might immediately and directly incite criminal acts.

This absolutist interpretation of the First Amendment was based on the now familiar but then novel and democratic theory that free government depends for its very existence and security on freedom of political discourse. The scope of the amendment was determined by the nature of the government and its relationship to the people. Since the government was their servant, existed by their consent and for their benefit, and was constitutionally limited, responsible, and elective, it could not, said Thomson, tell the citizens, "You shall not think this, or that upon certain subjects; or if you do, it is at your peril."[39] The concept of sedition could exist only in a relationship based on inferiority, when people were subjects rather than sovereigns and their criticism implied contempt of their master. "In the United States," Madison declared, "the case is altogether different."[40] Coercion or abridgment of unlimited political opinion, Wortman explained, would violate the very "principles of the social state," by which he meant a government of the people.[41] Because such a government depended upon popular elections, all the new libertarians agreed that the widest possible latitude must be maintained to keep the electorate free, informed, and capable of making intelligent choices. The citizen's freedom of political expression had the same scope as the legislator's, and for the same reasons.[42] Freedom might be dangerously abused, but the people would decide on men and measures wisely if exposed to every opinion.

The new libertarianism was complex, bold, original, and democratic.[43] It developed as an expediency of self-defense on the part of a besieged political minority struggling to maintain its existence and right to function unfettered. But it established a theory justifying the rights of individual expression and of opposition parties. In speeches, tracts, and books, George Blake, Albert Gallatin, Edward Livingston, Nathaniel Macon, James Madison, George Nicholas, John Thomson, St. George Tucker, and Tunis Wortman, among others, contributed brilliantly to the new theory of First Amendment freedoms.

Thomas Jefferson, however, contributed only tired clichés. The philosopher of freedom, unreflective and uninventive as a theorist, bound by the high-minded formulations of the Enlightenment, had his philosophy handed to him by his more liberal, more critical, followers. And it is doubtful that the new libertarianism meant much to Jefferson, for it scarcely altered his own thinking.

Jefferson's response to the Sedition Act contrasted markedly with that of the "Jeffersonians." He untiringly used the phrase "the freedom of the press," but he said little about it. He said a good deal, though, about states' rights. His Kentucky Resolutions of 1798, so often commended as a libertarian statement, included nine resolves, one of which dealt with freedom of the press. A paragraph in length—one of his most extended statements on the subject—it declared that the Constitution generally and the First Amendment particularly deprived the national government of any power over the press, reserving such power to the states. The bulk of the other resolves affirmed the principle of federalism as the reason for the unconstitutionality of the Sedition Act and its companion legislation. States' rights was the prime message of the Kentucky Resolutions. The Sedition Act was not void because a free, republican government could not punish the press for verbal crimes. It was void because the power to punish the crimes reached by the act "is reserved, and of right appertains, solely and exclusively, to the respective states, each within its own territory." It was void because the states "retain to themselves the right of judging how far the licentiousness of speech, and of the press, may be abridged without lessening their useful freedom."[44] Thus, to Jefferson, the First Amendment represented mainly an exclusive authority in the states to regulate speech and press.

Nor was Jefferson utilizing the federal principle simply as a tactical means of denying national authority. He believed in state control of the press, a fact that goes a long way to explain his pardon of the victims of the Sedition Act and his discontinuance of all pending prosecutions. That all the victims were his supporters was not without its influence. More interesting was his rationale for freeing Callendar and the other imprisoned editors. In a memorandum of 1801, he explained that he had abandoned the prosecution against William Duane, the Republican editor of the Philadelphia ***Aurora,*** because the case rested mainly on the unconstitutional Sedition Act. Jefferson wished "to secure to the press that degree of freedom in which it remained under the authority of the states, with whom alone the power is left of abridging that freedom, the general government being expressly excluded from it."[45]

Discussing Duane's case with Robert R. Livingston, a close friend, the new president showed how inattentive he was to the new libertarian theory of the press, when he wondered whether truth should not be a defense against a charge of seditious libel or contempt of Congress. "Have not the *Whig* lawyers of England," he asked —as if wholly ignorant of the very recent and powerful arguments of Republican lawyers in America—"always denied that the publication of truth could be either a contempt or a libel"? Regardless of English practice, did not the First Amendment free the printing of truth from a contempt charge; even if not, could he not, as President, pardon the offender?[46] In a letter to Gallatin, also discussing Duane's case, Jefferson suggested that a prosecution brought in the state court of Pennsylvania would have been lawful, "if any statute of that State, or statutory adoption of the common law of England, had made the offence punishable."[47] This was hardly a repudiation by Jefferson of the repressive law of seditious libel.

Repression was certainly not congenial to Jefferson's temperament or ideals. In 1802, he wrote to his attorney general, "I would wish much to see the experiment tried of getting along without public prosecutions for *libels.* I believe we can do it." Patience and good government, he thought, might make that experiment a success. Punishment was "impracticable" anyway, because juries could not be relied upon.[48] To a French correspondent, in 1803, he observed that it was difficult to draw a clear line between the abuse and the wholesome use of the press; "as yet," he added, "we have found it better to trust the public judgment, rather than the magistrate, with the discrimination between truth and falsehood."[49] These statements by no means reflected Jefferson's concurrence with the new libertarian doctrine that criminal prosecutions for false opinions or licentiousness should be abandoned. He had not at all relinquished the old concept of verbal crimes against the government. At best, he was keeping the government's claws retracted, hoping that the occasion would not arise for using them against the seditious.

Only two weeks after his letter to the French correspondent, Jefferson lost patience. He addressed an "entirely confidential" letter to Governor Thomas McKean of Pennsylvania, removing any doubt whether he believed that the states should exercise their power to punish seditious libels. The Federalists, he declared, having failed by the Sedition Act to destroy freedom of the press, had now attacked it by "pushing it's [*sic*] licentiousness & it's lying to such a degree of prostitution as to deprive it of all credit." The "tory presses" were so abandoned that the people could not believe what they read in the papers. For this situation Jefferson had a remedy:

> This is a dangerous state of things, and the press ought to be restored to it's [*sic*] credibility if possible. The restraints provided by the laws of the states are sufficient for this if applied. And I have therefore long thought that a few prosecutions of the most prominent offenders would have a wholesome effect in restoring the integrity of the presses. Not a general prosecution, for that would look like persecution; but a selected one. The paper I now inclose appears to me to offer as good an instance in every respect to make an example of, as can be selected . . . If the same thing be done in some other of the states it will place the whole band more on their guard.[50]

It is not surprising, therefore, that Jefferson did not protest when Pennsylvania prosecuted Joseph Dennie, the arch-Federalist editor of the Philadelphia *Port-Folio,* for seditious libel against the state and the United States.[51] Nor is it surprising that he remained silent when New York prosecuted Harry Croswell, editor of New York's Federalist paper, *The Wasp,* for the crime of seditiously libeling the President.[52]

In the year that Dennie and Croswell were indicted, Jefferson, in an article intended for anonymous publication in a Republican paper in Boston, mentioned that the "regulation of the press" was a subject "exclusively belonging to the state governments."[53] In the following year, 1804, when Abigail Adams criticized Jefferson for pardoning scoundrels who had been convicted under the Sedition Act in her husband's Administration, the President replied that he had acted in accordance with his belief that the statute exceeded the powers of the national government. "While we deny that Congress have a right to control the freedom of the press," he added, "we have ever asserted the right of the States, and their exclusive right, to do so." All the states had provisions for punishing "slander," he assured Mrs. Adams, and in general they appeared to have made the press responsible as far as was consistent with its "useful freedom." He did think, though, that a state would go "too far" if it did not permit truth as a defense.[54]

In 1805 Jefferson made public his opinion that libelous publications ought to be prosecuted. In his Second Inaugural Address, he noted that during "this course of administration, and in order to disturb it, the artillery of the press has been levelled against us, charged with whatsoever its licentiousness could devise or dare." Clearly, he was referring to seditious libels, not merely slander of private reputations. He regretted that the freedom of the press had been so misused. Its abuses "might, indeed, have been corrected by the wholesome punishments reserved and provided by the laws of the several States against falsehood and defamation," but urgent public duties, said the author of the confidential letter to Governor McKean, left little time for correcting the press by prosecutions. As a result, the world had witnessed a fair and full experiment whether truth might emerge in the course of free discussion, "unaided by power." Truth had indeed prevailed, for his re-election signified that the public judgment corrected false reasonings and opinions. "No inference is here intended," he added, "that the laws, provided by the State against false and defamatory publications, should not be enforced; he who has time, renders a service to public morals and public tranquillity, in reforming these abuses by the salutary coercions of the law."[55]

Not long after, Jefferson had occasion to condone one

of those salutary coercions, rather than leave the correction of false opinions to public judgment. The coercion, moreover, was undertaken by the federal rather than a state government, by a judge of Jefferson's own appointment, and under a federal common law of seditious libel which he himself, in the Kentucky Resolutions of 1798, had declared was "withheld from the cognizance of federal tribunals." A bitter political opponent described the event as Jefferson's "reign of terror" by "persecutions, wicked and despotic."[56]

The affair began with the President's appointment of Pierpont Edwards, in 1806, as United States District Judge for Connecticut. Edwards was one of the few Jeffersonian stalwarts in that fiercely Federalist state. Justice Paterson of the Supreme Court being ill, Judge Edwards conducted the United States Circuit Court alone, and he fixed on a course of political revenge. In an address of April 1806, to a grand jury hand-picked by a Republican marshal, Edwards asked for common-law indictments against the publishers of libels against the United States, on the ground that they would, if not restrained, "more effectually undermine and sap the foundations of our Constitution and Government, than any kind of treason that can be named."[57] The federal grand jurors returned indictments for seditious libel against Judge Tapping Reeve of the Connecticut Superior Court for articles he had published in the Litchfield *Monitor,* a Federalist paper; against Thomas Collier, publisher of the *Monitor;* and against Thaddeus Osgood, a candidate for the ministry. A few months later, Hudson and Goodwin, editors of the Federalist *Connecticut Courant* of Hartford, and the Reverend

Azel Backus were also indicted. The charge against each of the defendants was the same: seditious libel of President Jefferson. Backus and Osgood had committed the alleged crime in the course of preaching sermons; the other defendants in newspaper print.[58]

Jefferson, in 1809, informed a friend that the prosecutions "had been instituted, and had made considerable progress, without my knowledge, that they were disapproved by me *as soon as known,* and directed to be discontinued."[59] The prosecutions were doubtless instituted without Jefferson's knowledge, but he learned of them in December of 1806, nearly four months before they were scheduled for trial, and he did not disapprove of them until expediency forced him to do so some months later.

Thomas Seymour, a Connecticut Democrat, informed the President, in a letter of December 20, 1806, that the Republicans of Hartford backed the "prosecutions depending before the Circuit Court in this District, for Libels against the President and Administration of the General Government." He did not specify the character of the libels, but he apprised the President that the indictments had been returned by a grand jury of Judge Edwards' court, composed of "the most intelligent of our Citizens, attached to the principles which have uniformly guided the Administration." Without naming the defendants, he described them as "a Judge, two political Priests, and three Federal printers."[60] All Washington learned of the prosecutions when Connecticut Congressman Samuel W. Dana, who had already discussed them with a cabinet member—probably Gideon Granger—described them to the House of Representatives on January 2, 1807, in order to obtain support for his abortive bill making truth a defense in federal criminal libel trials.[61]

Jefferson himself replied to Seymour in a letter dated February 11, 1807, acknowledging the "prosecutions in the Court of the U S" and recommending that if truth be admitted as a defense, the effect could "not lessen the useful freedom of the press." He had never troubled to contradict the calumnies against him, he declared, and he would "leave to others"—Judge Pierpont Edwards and the United States jury?—the task of recalling the press to the truth.[62] Jefferson's letter to Seymour did not criticize the federal prosecutions, nor did he take any action to call a halt to them. At best he was aloof, but wished to avoid the embarrassment of a denial of the defense of truth under federal common-law proceedings, when even the hated Sedition Act of the Federalists had permitted defendants to prove their statements against the government. By a curious coincidence, Judge Edwards in Connecticut acted as if he "got the message." He shortly decided that section thirty-four of the Judiciary Act of 1789 required him to follow state law in common-law trials in the courts of the United States, with the consequence that a Connecticut statute of 1804 allowing truth as a defense was held to be applicable to the forthcoming trials.[63] This ruling ultimately undermined the government's position.

The case against Judge Reeve was not prosecuted because Judge Edwards, who was related to him by marriage, refused to issue a warrant of arrest. The trials of the other five defendants were scheduled for the April 1807 session of the court. The petty jurors were personally selected by the federal marshal instead of by lot as was customary. Defense counsel objected to the proceedings, stating that they intended to argue that the federal courts had no jurisdiction over crimes at common law. They also requested a postponement until Judge Edwards should be joined by a member of the Supreme Court on circuit duty.[64] For Judge Edwards, however, it was on-with-the-trials and off-with-their-heads. He ruled that it was against the peace of the state to let the cases lie over another year, because it was "improper the public mind should be kept in ferment as to the facts charged."[65] But his eagerness to try the cases immediately was frustrated by the discovery of defects in the indictments, resulting in the dismissal of the case against Thaddeus Osgood and a postponement of the other cases until the September 1807 session of the court.[66]

When the scheduled date for trial arrived, Edwards behaved in a manner that caused counsel for the defense to express "surprise at the unexpected turn the case had taken."[67] Upon receiving the expected renewal of demurrers from each of the defendants—except the Reverend Azel Backus—the judge promptly ruled that a decision on the plea to the court's jurisdiction should not be made until he was joined by a member of the Supreme Court. This ruling postponed the trials until the Supreme Court *en banc* finally determined whether the federal courts might exercise jurisdiction over common-law crimes. The Reverend Backus, however, insisted upon being tried immediately. His reputation, he argued, had been blackened by the indictment, and he therefore "was desirous of having the question upon the facts tried."[68] At that point a curious colloquy occurred between the judge and the defendant. The judge insistently—and quite inconsistently with his earlier rule in favor of immediate trial—sought to convince the defendant that it was not in his best interest to be tried, and even that the hardship and expense were avoidable should the jurisdictional point be ultimately decided in his favor. Backus remained adamant, however, and in the end his trial was indefinitely postponed against his protests.[69]

Judge Edwards had changed his mind between April and September about going ahead with the prosecutions. The explanation for his judicial somersault reveals why Backus was so eager to be tried. President Jefferson had learned for the first time the exact nature of Backus' libel. As he later recalled, "I heard of subpoenas being served on General [Henry] Lee, David M. Randolph, and others [from Virginia], as witnesses to attend the trial. I then for the first time conjectured the subject of the libel. I immediately wrote to Mr. Granger, to require an immediate dismission of the prosecution."[70] The libel in question concerned "the Walker affair" of 1768, when Jefferson seems to have attempted the seduction of a friend's wife. The incident had become a "public scandal" in 1805, as a result of the betrayal of the President by that notorious prostitute of journalism, James Callendar, and Jefferson had been forced to confess, to a member of his cabinet, the "incorrectness" of a long-forgotten fling at adultery: "when young and single I offered love to a handsome lady."[71]

Since the Reverend Backus had the facts on his side and had already subpoenaed the lady's husband, as well as James Madison and other Virginians, the decision to prevent the trial from coming off was understandable. But to have dismissed the prosecution against Backus only would have looked bad; even to have capitulated on all the cases would have placed the government in an unfavorable light. The course decided upon was to proceed with a test case that would draw from the Supreme Court a decision on the question whether the federal courts possessed common-law jurisdiction over criminal libels.

Accordingly in 1808 the government withdrew the prosecutions against Backus, Reeve, and Collier, but arranged for the appeal of the cases of Hudson and Goodwin, prior to trial, to the Supreme Court on their plea to the jurisdiction of the Circuit Court. The result was bizarre. Without hearing oral arguments (for counsel for the defense did not appear and neither did the Attorney General for the United States), in the face of about a dozen Circuit Court precedents—all of a kind—in which members of the Supreme Court had ruled in favor of common-law jurisdiction,[72] and against the unwritten dissenting opinions of only one less than a majority, Justice Johnson ruled very briefly that the United States courts might try only such crimes as were defined in the Constitution or Acts of Congress.[73] Thus ended the experiment of salutary coercion of the press by the Jefferson Administration.

After the chastening experience of the Backus case, Jefferson never again condoned criminal prosecutions for libel. He lost his faith, not in the principle of freedom of the press, but in the actual performance of the press. Now and again he alluded to the principle; more often he gave way to an outburst of revulsion, so deeply disappointed was he with the performance of the press in the United States. He had begun as the Enlightenment theorist, realistic enough to want safeguards against falsehoods when drafting or recommending constitutional provisions, but given to excessive enthusiasms about the indispensable functions of the press in a free society. "The basis of our governments," he wrote from Paris in 1787, "being the opinion of the people," public liberty depended upon public opinion; "were it left to me to decide whether we should have a government without newspapers, or newspapers without a government," he declared with as much foolishness as idealism, "I should not hesitate a moment to prefer the latter."[74]

By the time he left the presidency, a much wiser and embittered man, so convinced was he that the press was hopelessly abandoned to falsehoods and licentiousness—epithetical standards relinquished by libertarian theorists—that he professed to believe that it was doing more harm to the nation than would result from suppression.[75] "I deplore, with you," he wrote to a correspondent, "the putrid state into which our newspapers have passed, and the malignity, the vulgarity, and mendacious spirit of those who write for them; and I enclose you a recent sample . . . as a proof of the abyss of degradation into which we have fallen. These ordures," he exclaimed—forgetting that the press mirrored American culture and the people whom he professed, in moments of intellectual isolation, to trust—"are rapidly depraving the public taste, and lessening its relish for sound food. As vehicles of information, and a curb on our functionaries, they have rendered themselves useless, by forfeiting all title to belief."[76] The violence and malignity of party spirit, he thought, was the cause of the press's fall from grace.

Jefferson's diagnosis of the ills of the press lacked a realistic understanding of partisan politics. Coming from the man who had backed the savage partisanship of Bache, Callendar, Freneau, Ritchie, and Taylor, from the 1790's to the 1820's, his characterization of the press would not have been admitted into a court of equity where the doctrine of "clean hands" prevailed. Moreover, the press was not nearly as bad as Jefferson depicted it. There were several good papers, all strongly partisan to be sure and all given to excesses in characterizing men and measures in matters of politics. On balance, though, the *National Intelligencer* in Washington and *Niles' Weekly Register* in Baltimore reflected credit on American journalism, while there were many papers —Boston's *Independent Chronicle* and *Columbian Centinel;* New York's *National Advocate, Evening Post,* and *Commercial Advertiser;* Baltimore's *American;* and Richmond's *Enquirer,* among others—that were as fair and responsible as any that Jefferson had ever seen. The press, as a matter of fact, improved in quality during his lifetime. He, however, grew more sour and depressed about the press, finally giving it up as altogether hopeless.

In later life Jefferson read only one paper, the Richmond *Enquirer,* "and in that chiefly the advertisements, for they contain the only truths to be relied on in a newspaper."[77] A few years later, when his opinion of American newspapers had not changed,[78] he wrote a stirring, yet in some respects a pathetic, letter to a Frenchman in which he extolled the virtues of a free press. It was as if his mind had gone back to the exciting, hopeful period when he was in Paris in the 1780's. France, he had heard, had formed a new government that had not yet framed a constitution. The American experience, he wrote with pride, might serve as a model. The several state constitutions had bills of rights that embodied principles essential to personal and public liberty, and deserving of France's consideration. Among these principles was:

> freedom of the press, subject only to liability for personal injuries. This formidable censor of the public functionaries, by arraigning them at the tribunal of public opinion, produces reform peaceably, which must otherwise be done by revolution. It is also the best instrument for enlightening the mind of man, and improving him as a rational, moral, and social being.[79]

The remark catapulted Jefferson into the ranks of the most advanced libertarians, for no one had ever advocated a wider freedom than that which was restrained only by liability for "personal injuries." But it was a jarring remark, unique in his thinking about the press and, significantly, not written for home consumption. It was, nevertheless, the wisest remark he ever made on the subject. Coming as it did in 1823, it was his final testament on freedom of the press—a reflex of the best Enlightenment theory.[80]

✧ Chapter Four ✧

A Dictatorship in Extreme Cases: The Burr Conspiracy

In the closing years of his presidency, the Burr conspiracy and the embargo fixed Jefferson's attention. On both subjects he was insensible to constitutional limitations and to standards of fairness. Had Timothy Pickering masterminded the Administration's conduct of the Burr case, it would not have been remarkable. But Thomas Jefferson was responsible. The President of the United States, in a special message to Congress, gave the nation to understand that a citizen who just a few weeks earlier had been exonerated by a federal grand jury was guilty of high treason. On the basis of "little" that constituted "formal and legal evidence," chiefly letters "often containing such a mixture of rumors, conjectures, and suspicions, as render it difficult to sift out the real facts," Jefferson announced that Burr, at the head of military enterprise, had sought "the severance of the Union." He had planned to seize New Orleans, plunder its wealth and military supplies, use it to detach the West beyond the Alleghenies, and conquer Mexico. Burr's guilt, concluded Jefferson, "is placed beyond all question."[1] Whether Burr's criminal enterprise was a filibuster against the territory of a friendly nation, or treason against the United States, or a conspiracy to commit treason, is quite beside the point. John Adams made the point simply enough: "But if his [Burr's] guilt is as clear as the Noon day Sun, the first Magistrate ought not to have pronounced it so before a Jury had tryed him."[2]

Having convicted Burr before the bar of public opinion prior to his apprehension, the first Magistrate proceeded relentlessly to mobilize executive resources to prove the preconceived guilt. Jefferson did not turn the case over to the United States attorney, but acted himself as prosecutor, superintending the gathering of evidence, locating witnesses, taking depositions, directing trial tactics, and shaping public opinion as if judge and juror for the nation.[3]

The object was not to secure justice by having Burr's guilt—or innocence—fairly determined, but to secure a conviction, no matter how, on the charge of high treason. To do so, it became necessary to accept unquestioningly the word of a Spanish spy and master of mendacious duplicity, James Wilkinson, the commanding general of the United States Army. It became necessary to justify Wilkinson's outrageously illegal acts of military tyranny and to join in assaulting the integrity and patriotism of the judiciary. It became necessary to recommend a constitutional amendment to make the judges subservient to the political branches of the government, on pain of recall. It became necessary to believe that prejudiced persons should serve as grand jurors, that mere suspicion of the accused warranted a trial for his life, that the presidential word of honor should be broken without scruple and a witness betrayed in order to obtain needed testimony.

Jefferson's handling of the interrogation and proceedings against Dr. Eric Bollman illuminated his conduct in the case. Bollman, who was one of Burr's principal aides, had been illegally arrested by the military and transported from New Orleans to the East to stand trial for treason. Escorted from prison by a squad of soldiers to be interviewed by the President and Secretary of State, Bollman was eager to talk. Jefferson expected to get from him a full confession of Burr's treasonable plans. But the prisoner denied that there had been any conspiracy to seize New Orleans or to sever the West from the Union. He confessed that the object of the plot was to conquer Mexico and urged that the United States declare war on Spain, a measure that would have been immensely popular in the West.[4] Bollman admitted that there had been a good deal of talk about a revolution in Louisiana, but all for the purpose of duping the Spanish by directing their attention from Burr's true objective.

Bollman's confession had been given after the President had voluntarily assured him that nothing he said would be used as evidence to incriminate him. Though Madison had taken notes, Jefferson requested Bollman to put his remarks in writing. The President's letter offered *"his word of honour* that they shall never be used against himself [Bollman], and *that the paper shall never go out of his hand."*[5] Bollman promptly furnished the President with a signed statement of almost twenty pages.

Within a month, Chief Justice Marshall freed Bollman on a writ of habeas corpus, ruling that there was no evidence to warrant his being held on a charge of treason.[6] But the President was not finished with Bollman whom he meant to use as a witness against Burr or, failing that, to imprison. When the case for an indictment against the archconspirator was prepared, the President sent Bollman's signed statement to the United States attorney, George Hay, in Richmond. Noting that Bollman's statement had been made with the assurance that it "should never be used *against himself*," Jefferson informed Hay that it would be useful "that you may know how to examine him, and draw everything from him." If Bollman lied on the stand, Hay "should go so far as to ask him whether he did not say so and so to Mr. Madison and myself." To induce Bollman to testify, Jefferson enclosed a pardon. If Bollman refused to appear as a witness, he was to be taken immediately into custody.[7] A week later Jefferson modified his instructions to Hay. "On further reflection," he declared, "I think you may go farther, if he prevaricates grossly, and shew the paper to him, and ask if it is not his handwriting, and confront him by its contents."[8]

Bollman proved too hard a nut for the government to crack. Although Hay used his statement against him in court, made it available to Wilkinson, and made its contents known, Bollman refused to incriminate Burr or himself. On the stand he declared his innocence and indignantly rejected the proffered presidential pardon as an insulting assumption of his guilt.[9] In a rage, the President ordered Hay to move "to commit him immediately for treason or misdemeanor."[10]

Jefferson also claimed that he had found a witness in Baltimore who could testify that it was "believed" for some time in that city that Burr "was engaged in some criminal enterprise, and that Luther Martin knew all about it." Martin, who was one of Burr's defense counsels, had been making the President look like Caligula. "Shall we move to commit Luther Martin as *particeps criminis* with Burr?" asked Jefferson. "Graybell [the Baltimore witness who was never again heard of] will fix upon him misprision of treason at least. And at any rate, his evidence will put down this unprincipled and impudent federal bulldog, and add another proof that the most clamorous defenders of Burr are all his accomplices."[11] However, the court's requirement of evidence proving guilt beyond reasonable doubt rather than mere belief of guilt blocked Jefferson's impulse to imprison anyone who stood in his way by supporting Burr.

Jefferson was disappointed even in his desire to have the government's case against Burr submitted to a grand jury composed exclusively of men friendly to the Administration. William Branch Giles, the Administration leader in the Senate, and Wilson Cary Nicholas, his predecessor in that position, had been challenged by Burr's counsel as hostile or biased, and both voluntarily withdrew as grand jurors.[12] To Hay, the prosecutor, who had conceded Burr's right to challenge grand jurors,[13] Jefferson angrily wrote that Giles and Nicholas were "as far above all exception as any two persons in the U.S."; correcting Hay on proper procedure, Jefferson informed him—alas too late—that challenge and rejection in the case of grand jurors is "impossible."[14] To his son-in-law, Congressman John W. Eppes, Jefferson lamented, "A grand jury of 2 feds, 4 Quids and 10 republicans does not seem to be a fair representation of the state of Virginia."[15] This enumeration of the grand jurors by their political affiliation stiffened the credibility of Andrew Jackson's comment that the trial of Burr "assumed the shape of a political persecution."[16]

Burr, who deserved little sympathy, conducted himself admirably at his prosecution. His view of the grand jury, as contrasted with that of the President, was striking. When, for example, one of the grand jurors requested to be excused from duty because he had formed an opinion against Burr, the defendant remarked that the grand juror's candor permitted the hope that he might endeavor to be impartial. Burr would not, therefore, object to him, nor did Burr object to another grand juror who also admitted "sentiments unfavourable to Colonel Burr."[17] Burr received a fair trial under Chief Justice Marshall, but the dubious nature of the evidence and irregularities in the prosecution, some of them gross and shocking, discredited the Administration.

Had the President been convinced that Burr was guilty of treason and threatened the security of the nation, his handling of the case would still be inexcusable, although understandable. But there is doubt whether the President, despite his frenetic efforts to obtain a conviction, was convinced that Burr was the American Catiline. As late as April 20, 1807, Jefferson admitted to Senator Giles that the government might not be able to prove overt acts of treason. He added, "we do not know of a certainty yet what will be proved."[18] This statement was made three weeks after the government had moved to hold Burr for the grand jury on a charge of treason, and three months after the public proclamation that Burr was guilty "beyond all doubt." Either Jefferson sought a conviction for treason in the face of his own doubt about Burr's guilt, or irresponsibly flirted with doctrines of constructive treason by playing fast and loose with the law of evidence as well as with criminal procedures.

Jefferson was furious when Chief Justice Marshall held Burr on a charge of high misdemeanor for attempting to levy war against Mexico, but refused to hold him on the major charge of levying war against the United States. Marshall distinguished the act of treason from a conspiracy to commit it or an intent to do so. He demanded proof that the crime of treason had in fact been committed and that the accused was probably guilty. The charge of treason, the most serious that could be brought against a citizen, had been historically abused as an instrument of "malignant and vindictive" tyrannies. Consequently, declared the Chief Justice, the framers of the Constitution, wisely denying the government the discretionary power to define treason, explicitly provided that it meant only the levying of war against the United States, or adhering to its enemies by giving them aid and comfort. Moreover, the character of the proof had also been constitutionally defined: testimony to the overt act by two witnesses. It would be dangerous, Marshall concluded, to extend the crime "by construction" to doubtful cases. Since no proof had been produced to show Burr's probable guilt, or even to show that the crime itself had been committed, the prisoner could not be held for the grand jury on charge of treason.[19]

Jefferson immediately responded with a proposition alien to the common law and hazardous to personal liberty: "Hitherto we have believed our law to be, that suspicion on probable grounds was sufficient cause to commit a person for trial."[20] Jefferson, in other words, was satisfied with mere probable suspicion as to the accused's guilt, whereas the law required proof of probable guilt before commitment and a prima facie case of guilt before trial. The law also required absolute proof that the crime itself had been committed; Jefferson wanted Burr put to trial for treason without the crime itself having been established.

Bad law on the part of the President, in a case for a capital crime, and a political one at that, was infinitely more dangerous in view of what he considered proofs of the overt acts of treason. There were, of course, overt acts, such as the enlistment and arming of men at Blennerhasset's Island, but whether they were treason was very dubious. Certainly the chief justice and the jury found them wanting. The case presented by the government at the trial was not unreasonable; but the case as it existed in Jefferson's mind was in many respects simply farfetched.

"And as to the overt acts," Jefferson asked rhetorically, "were not the bundle of letters of information in Mr. Rodney's hands, the letters and facts published in the local newspapers, Burr's flight, and the universal belief or rumor of his guilt, probable ground for presuming . . . overt acts to have taken place?"[21] The letters referred to as being in the attorney general's possession were the accusations from the mendacious Wilkinson, who richly deserved to be in Burr's place, and from William Eaton who had implicated Wilkinson and recommended Burr for an ambassadorship to get him out of the country. Eaton's tale of treasons was exhumed, when Jefferson realized that Wilkinson's letters were insufficient to hold Burr's accomplices, Bollman and Swartwout.[22]

As for the newspaper stories, which as evidence were less than hearsay, Jefferson's own dictum of 1807 was: "Nothing can now be believed which is seen in a newspaper . . . I will add, that the man who never looks into a newspaper is better informed than he who reads them; inasmuch as he who knows nothing is nearer to truth than he whose mind is filled with falsehoods and errors."[23]

That Jefferson would have had a federal court in a treason case accept as evidence of overt acts the alleged "universal belief or rumor" of guilt showed the degree to which he would pervert the law and adopt the doctrine of constructive treason. Indeed, if he meant what he said, he was prepared to "presume" on merely "probable" grounds the existence of the overt acts which were necessary to prove the crime.

Nor was Burr's flight an additional proof. Burr as recently as February of 1807 had surrendered voluntarily to the civil authorities in Mississippi Territory, had readily submitted to a federal grand jury investigation, had been completely exonerated of "any crime or misdemeanor against the laws of the United States or of this Territory,"[24] and after walking out of court a free man, had learned that a military patrol was on its way to arrest him. Only then did he flee to escape illegal arrest, perhaps assassination. As a matter of fact, Wilkinson had sent civilians and several officers in disguise to capture Burr. He had even offered a reward of $5000 to one Silas Dinsmore should he succeed, and payment of his expenses in case of failure.[25] Under the circumstances, Burr, who never avoided an investigation by civil authorities, had been well advised by friends to escape. That Jefferson cited his flight as proof of guilt proved more than the flimsiness of the government's evidence. It proved, like the willingness to use rumor and newspaper accounts, that Jefferson's lax concept of treason smelled of the English doctrines of the seventeenth century that he himself had repudiated during the Revolution.

Jefferson's view was that the courts were protecting traitors. Years earlier, in 1789, when Jefferson was attempting to convince Madison of the value of a Bill of Rights, he wrote that one argument which had "great weight" was "the legal check which it puts into the hands of the judiciary. This is a body, which if rendered independent, and kept strictly to their own department merits great confidence for their learning and integrity. In fact what degree of confidence would be too much for a body composed of such men as Wythe, Blair and Pendleton? On characters like these the *'civium ardor prava jubentium'* [wayward zeal of the ruling citizens] would make no impression."[26] In 1807 when Chief Justice Marshall enforced legal and constitutional standards, checking the zeal of the ruling citizen, the President persistently railed against the "error in our Constitution, which makes any branch independent of the nation." Since impeachment was a "farce," he wrote, an amendment was needed to rebuke the judiciary for extending "immunity to that class of offenders which endeavors to overturn the Constitution, and are themselves protected in it by the Constitution . . . If their protection of Burr produces this amendment, it will do more good than his condemnation would have done."[27]

That was Jefferson's reaction to Marshall's refusal at the preliminary hearing to hold Burr on a treason charge without probable cause.

When the grand jury was formed it included ten loyal or Administration Republicans, just two short of the necessary dozen votes to indict. Jefferson observed that his party was unfairly represented, proving "the original error of establishing a judiciary independent of the nation, and which, from the citadel of the law can turn it's [*sic*] guns on those they were meant to defend."[28] After Burr's acquittal Jefferson declared once again that the result was "equivalent to a proclamation of impunity to every traitorous combination which may be formed to destroy the Union," but an amendment to the Constitution would make the judiciary dependent on the "nation."[29]

In his Seventh Annual Message, the President originally included a line, later struck out, stating that "whenever the laws were appealed to in aid of the public safety, their operation was on behalf of those only against whom they were invoked." He did not strike out an invitation to Congress to judge for itself whether Burr had been acquitted because of a defect in the evidence, in the law, or its administration by the judiciary, and to apply a remedy—a recommendation for a constitutional amendment checking the courts. "The framers of our constitution," he concluded ominously, "certainly supposed they had guarded, as well their government against destruction by treason, as their citizens against oppression under pretence of it: and if these ends are not obtained, it is of importance to enquire by what means, more effectual, they may be secured."[30]

The amendment recommended by Jefferson throughout 1807 had originally been proposed by John Randolph, first in 1805 and again in 1806. It made federal judges removable by the President on the joint address of both houses of Congress.[31] A few days after Jefferson's Seventh Annual Address, Senator Edward Tiffin of Ohio offered the same amendment, with the additional provision that the judges' tenure be limited to a specified number of years.[32] The proposed amendment however was never reported out of committee. Jefferson's goal of checking the judiciary failed. His advocacy in 1789 of an independent judiciary as a means of enforcing civil liberties against the goverment better comports with the image of him as the apostle of freedom.

Through the whole period of his agitation about Burr, Jefferson gave undeviating support to Wilkinson's despotic rule in New Orleans. The general entered New Orleans a few days after dispatching to Mexico City an emissary who carried information detailing Wilkinson's opposition to Burr's conspiracy and requesting more than $121,000 for services rendered to Spain.[33] In short order Wilkinson had New Orleans quaking in panic over an expected invasion by Burr. Traitors were everywhere; conquest, plunder, murder, and a slave revolt were imminent. "Under circumstances so imperious," he informed Governor William C. Claiborne, "extraordinary measures must be resorted to and the ordinary form of civil institutions must for a short period yield to the strong arm of military law." Suspension of the writ of habeas corpus and proclamation of martial law —turning New Orleans over to Wilkinson—were the only means of saving the city, he argued, for he must be authorized "to repress the seditious and arrest the disaffected."[34] When Claiborne persisted in the view that he was powerless to comply with these demands, in the absence of legislative authorization, the general summarily took matters into his own hands and acted as if martial law had been declared. He unleashed a saturnalia of lawlessness.

Samuel Swartwout and Peter V. Ogden, who were Burr's couriers, and Eric Bollman, Burr's intermediary with Wilkinson, were arrested without warrants and held incommunicado, their papers confiscated, access to counsel and the courts denied them. Writs of habeas corpus were issued the next day on their behalf, compelling Wilkinson and his officers to show cause within twenty-four hours why they held their prisoners. But the local court could not save Bollman and Swartwout. Wilkinson bound them in chains in a ship's brig and gave the orders that sent them seaward to Washington under military escort. To the court Wilkinson sent an aide with his reply to the writ of habeas corpus: "The commander of the army of the United States takes on himself all the responsibility which may result from the arrest of Eric Bollman, who is accused of being guilty of the crime of treason . . . and I have taken opportune measures to warrant his safe delivery into the hands of the President . . . I shall arrest without respect to class or station all those against whom I have positive proof of being accomplices in the machinations against the state."[35]

Ogden, who had not been imprisoned on ship, was produced in court, after Governor Claiborne interceded on his behalf, and was freed on the ground that there was no evidence against him. But within twenty-four hours he and James Alexander, an attorney whose only crime was to apply for a writ of habeas corpus for Ogden, were arrested by the military, spirited out of the court's jurisdiction, and secretly transported by sea to Washington. When writs of habeas corpus were sued out on their behalf, Wilkinson informed the court that his answer in the case of Bollman was "applicable to the traitors who are the subjects of this writ."[36] The judge, James Workman, vigorously assailing the general's defiance, insistently sought Governor Claiborne's support and that of the legislature against the "lawless measures" of the territory's "oppressor." Wilkinson answered by condemning the judge and a friend, Lewis Kerr, for being "actively engaged in these nefarious projects," and arrested them both.

The editor of the *Orleans Gazette* was also arrested, and the federal post office was rifled by Wilkinson's men searching for "incriminating" evidence. In January of 1807 Wilkinson seized General John Adair without warrant and denied him the writ of habeas corpus. A month later, Lieutenant Robert T. Spence became Wilkinson's victim. Adair and Spence were both shipped off to Washington. In Natchez, right after Burr's flight from that vicinity, Wilkinson's dragnet closed in on about sixty others, though only a few were committed for trial and all, like Judge Workman, were eventually acquitted or their cases nol-prossed.[37]

Jefferson's reaction to his general's conduct in New Orleans was to applaud a job well done. Wilkinson had sent several dispatches relating his military preparations and seizure of traitors. The President, in his answer, tactfully explained that Burr's army was descending the Mississippi from Nashville with only eighty to one hundred men in boats navigated by sixty oarsmen "not at all of his party." Wilkinson's alarmed warning that Burr commanded six or seven thousand men was therefore unfounded, explained the President, but the general was justified in his vigorous defense operations.

Turning to Wilkinson's arrests, Jefferson wrote: "Your sending here Swartwout and Bollman, and adding to them Burr, Blannerhasset [*sic*], and Tyler, should they fall into your hands, will be supported by the public opinion." But disturbed by the fact that the evidence received against Alexander and Ogden would not be sufficient to hold them, Jefferson added, "I hope, however, you will not extend this deportation to persons against whom there is only suspicion, or shades of offence not strongly marked. In that case, I fear the public sentiment would desert you; because, seeing no danger here, violations of law are felt with strength."[38]

Thus Jefferson measured Wilkinson's arrests by neither legal nor moral standards, but only by the extent to which public opinion would support them. He assured his general that despite "a good deal of malicious insinuation" against him in the press, begetting suspicion and distrust from those who did not know his "line of conduct," those who knew it "have not failed to strengthen the public confidence in you; and I can assure you that your conduct, as now known, has placed you on ground extremely favorable with the public."[39]

On the day that he wrote this letter to Wilkinson, the President also passed on to Governor Claiborne his judgment that military arrests in time of crisis were just if supported by public opinion. "On great occasions," wrote the President, "every good officer must be ready to risk himself in going beyond the strict line of law, when the public preservation requires it . . . The Feds, and the little band of Quids, in opposition, will try to make something of the infringement of liberty by the military arrest and deportation of citizens, but if it does not go beyond such offenders as Swartwout, Bollman, Burr, Blennerhasset, Tyler, etc., they will be supported by the public approbation."[40] Years earlier, when writing the Declaration of Independence, Jefferson had thought that among George III's serious crimes were those making the "Military independent of and superior to the Civil Power" and "transporting us beyond Seas to be tried."

President Jefferson in 1807 was right in believing that the opposition would not ignore the infringement of liberty. The Senate supported him, but his own party in the House proved embarrassing. In his message to Congress, on January 22, declaring Burr's guilt, he noted that according to Wilkinson's latest dispatches three of Burr's "principal emissaries" had been apprehended. One, he said, had been liberated by habeas corpus, but the other two "have been embarked" for Atlantic ports, "probably on the consideration that an impartial trial could not be expected" in New Orleans—a misleading explanation of Wilkinson's deportation of his prisoners in violation of the right to trial by a jury of the vicinage. The "first regular arrest," added the President, would occur "here"—a candid acknowledgment that the original arrests had been irregular, to say the least—and the prisoners would be turned over to the civil authorities for trial.[41]

On receiving this message, the Senate, the following day, acted with unbelievable haste to please the President. His message was read as a hint that the prisoners would surely be freed on writs of habeas corpus as soon as military jurisdiction over them ended. By unanimous consent, on a motion from Giles of Virginia, the Senate rules were "dispensed with" and a bill was quickly passed, without debate, suspending the writ of habeas corpus for three months in all cases of persons charged with treason or other high crimes against the United States and arrested or imprisoned on authority of the President or anyone acting under his direction (for example, Wilkinson).[42]

Only Senator Bayard of Delaware voted against the bill which was presented to the House "in confidence," with a request for emergency action. But the House balked at having the bill crammed down its throat and in being advised to deliberate in secret. In a public debate the House whipped the Senate bill from pillar to post as an unconscionable and wholly needless violation of the Constitution. A bipartisan majority of 113 to 19 then voted down the measure.[43] Jefferson, "presuming" that the bill suspending the writ of habeas corpus would pass, had already instructed the United States attorney for the District of Columbia to apply for a bench warrant against Bollman and Swartwout.[44] Jefferson may not have asked for the bill, but the Senate surely and reasonably expected that he would sign it into law if it passed.[45]

Party lines were shortly re-formed when Representative Jacob Broom, a Delaware Federalist, moved a bill "to make further provision for securing the privilege of the writ of habeas corpus to persons in custody under or by color of the authority of the United States."[46] Ogden and Alexander, at this time, had already been freed by habeas corpus, but Adair's case was yet to be decided, and Bollman and Swartwout had lost on their application for the writ in the United States District Court. Before Chief Justice Marshall could rule on their appeals and free them for want of evidence, the House treated itself to a three-day party donnybrook over the writ of habeas corpus and Wilkinson's arbitrary conduct in New Orleans. The "Feds and Quids" made the most of the edifying spectacle of the President's party, critics of the Sedition Act, opposing a strengthening of the great writ of constitutional liberty and justifying violations of fundamental law by bayonet rule. Although the Administration's conduct was subjected remorselessly to bruising criticism, the House finally voted on "indefinite postponement" of Broom's bill, sixty to fifty-eight.[47]

As 1807 wore on into springtime, the full story of New Orleans' experience under Wilkinson became public. In March the territorial legislature in New Orleans formally remonstrated to Congress. The events of the preceding December and January, when civil authority had been subverted, were vividly depicted. Violent measures, the remonstrance concluded, might be justified in moments of extreme danger, such as an imminent invasion, "But here no foreign enemy or open domestic foe was then, or has yet proved to have been within any perilous distance of this city, or that treason lurked without our walls . . . The acts of high-handed military power to which we have been exposed [are] acts too notorious to be denied, too illegal to be justified, too wanton to be excused."[48]

Jefferson may have heard only Wilkinson's side of the story when he had congratulated him on doing his duty and assured him that public opinion would approve of his conduct. But the President knew soon enough the other side. Yet his opinion of Wilkinson's conduct only stiffened in the case of criticism. He found ways to justify the illegal and excuse the wanton, rather than deny the notorious. In private Jefferson seems to have denied only the undeniable fact that Burr's arrest had been made by military authority. To Captain Edmund Pendleton Gaines, of all people, the man who actually captured Burr and arrested him without warrant, on the authority of the President, Jefferson wrote, five months after the arrest: "That the arrest of Colonel Burr was military has been disproved; but had it been so, every honest man and good citizen is bound, by any means in his power, to arrest the author of projects so daring and dangerous."[49]

In June the President sympathized with his favorite general on having undergone a "fiery trial" at New Orleans. Blindly Jefferson wrote that "it was soon apparent that the clamorous were only the criminal"[50]—this, after the congressional debates, after the remonstrance of the territorial legislature, and after the scathing words of the federal courts in issuing writs of habeas corpus to every prisoner seized and transported by Wilkinson![51] After Burr had been acquitted, Jefferson demonstrated that he had learned nothing from the critics or from the courts; indeed, that his resolution to support Wilkinson had become unshakable. On October 27, 1807, he expressed disappointment that "these people" did not "get what they deserved." It was then that he discoursed on the inapplicability of invoking "forms of the law to cover traitors," and on the necessity in "extreme cases" of resorting to "a dictator, or martial law." He added, to be sure, that in Washington it was understood that the danger apprehended by Wilkinson was unjustified. From the general's view in New Orleans, however, "it was reasonable according to the state of information there, to act on the expectation of daily attack."[52]

Jefferson's argument was objectionable on constitutional and libertarian grounds, even on grounds of fact. He should have known that it was not reasonable on the basis of information available in New Orleans to expect an attack. The danger was a figment of the general's imagination. Governor Claiborne knew that, although he had finally buckled before *force majeure;* the legislature in New Orleans had known it and said so during and after the pretended crisis; as early as February 21, 1807, Senator William Plumer had known it and recorded in his journals that it was very apparent to public opinion in Washington that "Wilkinson himself has created much of the alarm, & has greatly exaggerated the force & importance of Burr."[53]

Even if it had been true that Wilkinson had really believed that an attack on the city by Burr was imminent, though Burr was hundreds of miles away, Jefferson had not answered John Randolph's charge. On the floor of Congress the leader of the Quids had called attention to the fact that the Constitution permitted only Congress to suspend the writ of habeas corpus. To condone Wilkinson's conduct, declared Randolph, meant to read the constitutional safeguard as if it said, the writ of habeas corpus shall not be suspended "unless in the opinion of a military commander, it be necessary!"[54] An even more incisive reply to Jefferson had been made by Representative James Elliot of Vermont. He had heard enough, he declared, about the wisdom and republican virtue of the Administration. "From the same quarter we are told that the *salus populi* may have required and may justify the *lex suprema* of military despotism. This doctrine is unknown to the Constitution. That sacred record of our rights proclaims itself and itself alone . . . the *lex suprema,* the 'supreme law of the land.' It acknowledges no superior. It contemplates no case in which the law of arms can erect a throne upon its ruins."[55]

The opinion furthest removed from Jefferson's defense of dictatorship in extreme cases was expressed by Jefferson himself many years earlier, in 1781, immediately after his retirement as governor of Virginia. The state at the time was overrun by a British invasion under Generals Arnold and Cornwallis. The prospects of independent survival never seemed dimmer. At the instigation of Patrick Henry, Jefferson's own weakness as a war governor was under investigation by the Assembly. That body was also seriously considering the desperate expedient, on the ancient precedent of the Roman Republic, of resorting to a dictator. Richard Henry Lee, in a panic, urged Congress to vest General Washington "with Dictatorial power," and send him immediately to Virginia. Others favored General Nathaniel Greene or Patrick Henry. General Thomas Nelson, Jr., the highest ranking member of the Virginia militia, was finally elected to succeed Jefferson, "and the Assembly actually went a considerable distance toward military dictatorship by vesting Nelson with powers which Jefferson never had and would not have wanted."[56]

Under these circumstances, Jefferson wrote the chapter on "Constitution," later published in his *Notes on the State of Virginia.* Several impassioned pages were devoted to the recent proposal of June 1781, which "wanted a few votes only of being passed," to create a "dictator." Jefferson wrote in the immediate aftermath of a "calamity" to the state and nation that made the Burr conspiracy, by comparison, seem like a trivial incident devoid of danger.

If he was right in 1781, and he was never more right, he was never more wrong nor more faithless to libertarian principles than in 1807 and 1808. "One who entered into this contest from a pure love of liberty," he declared in 1781, "and a sense of injured rights, who determined to make every sacrifice, and to meet every danger, for the re-establishment of those rights on a firm basis, who did not mean to expend his blood and substance for the wretched purpose of changing this master for that" must stand confounded and dismayed when told that his rights were to be surrendered into a single hand and the people be delivered to a despotic one. "In God's name," he exclaimed, "from whence have they derived this power? . . . Is it from any principle in our new constitution, expressed or implied? Every lineament of that expressed or implied, is in full opposition to it." The fundamental principle of the state constitution was popular government which "proscribes . . . the exercise of all powers undefined by the laws."

Waxing to his subject, Jefferson refuted the precedent drawn from ancient Rome. History showed, he explained, that the experiment had proved fatal to liberty. The very thought of a dictator, even on a temporary basis and by whatever name he be called, "was treason against the people; was treason against mankind in general; as rivetting for ever the chains which bow down their necks, by giving to their oppressors a proof, which they would have trumpeted through the universe, of the imbecility of republican government, in times of pressing danger, to shield them from harm."[57]

By Governor Jefferson's standards, President Jefferson's rationalization of General Wilkinson's conduct betrayed the people. Yet Jefferson's mature judgment in the case of James Wilkinson never altered. Reflecting on the affair from the vantage of retirement at Monticello, he declared that a strict observance of the written laws was a high duty, "but it is not *the highest.*" The unwritten laws of necessity, of self-preservation, of saving the country, were the highest. In Wilkinson's case, he declared, consideration must be given to the fact that Burr was expected to attack, and there was a "formidable conspiracy" within the city. On the question whether Wilkinson was justified in seizing the conspirators, "there can be but two opinions; one, of the guilty and their accomplices; the other, that of all honest men." On the question whether he was justified in sending them to Washington "when the written law gave them a right to trial in the territory," the answer again hangs on the state of affairs in New Orleans, which imposed "a law of necessity and self-preservation, and rendered the *salus populi* supreme over the written law."[58] Thus, Jefferson closed the Burr conspiracy and the case of Wilkinson deeply convinced that his own conduct and that of Wilkinson had throughout been dictated by the highest considerations of national security, the Constitution notwithstanding.

✧ Chapter Five ✧

Passive Resistance Enforced by Bayonets: The Embargo, I

Soon after the Burr-conspiracy prosecutions the Administration's embargo policy engrossed the nation's attention. The two mightiest powers in the world had been guilty of acts warranting a declaration of war by the United States. It was a noble dream to attempt to use pacific sanctions against them. The Association of the Revolutionary period and the brief embargo of 1794 suggested to Jefferson an alternative to war. But never before had economic coercion been tried, as an instrument of national policy, on so vast a scale and without a time limit on the experiment. It proved impossible to persuade England or France against their military interests to respect American maritime rights in return for a restoration of American trade.

The success of the embargo depended ultimately on the willingness of a free people to suffer acute economic privation for a great national goal. Widespread coercion of Americans to enforce a policy of passive resistance resulted in failure of the policy. Jefferson needed more than a substitute for war; he also needed a substitute for the patriotic behavior stimulated by war. Passive resistance on a national scale required the arousing of a popular fervor for voluntary compliance. Coercion, of Americans as well as foreign nations, was an inescapable reality of the experiment; but success hung on the degree and kind of coercion. The task of the President was to enlist the support of the nation by educating the people on the need for complying with unusually onerous laws.

Except for the irreconcilables who supported the Essex Junto, the majority of Federalist voters were loyal American citizens, little different from their Republican counterparts. The sacrifices expected of all American citizens could have been explained by the President. Means of softening, even compensating for, the impact of the embargo, particularly upon the economy of the Northeast and the port towns, might have been sought. Proof that the embargo was intended against Napoleon as well as against England might have allayed suspicions sown by the pro-English, antiembargo Essex Junto.[1] Enforcement of the embargo, to insure its success, would under no circumstances have been easy. But a "war" by the government against a substantial minority of the American people was avoidable. Careful planning and democratic, but firm, presidential leadership, taking the people into confidence rather than taking them for granted, might have given the embargo policy a chance of success. In each respect Jefferson failed. The policy itself may have been admirable, but the manner of its adoption, execution, and defeat, for which he was responsible, was not.

From the beginning of the embargo throughout fifteen months of agonizing national trial, Jefferson's conduct impaired public liberty—and the success of his own policy as well. The embargo was the plan of an idealist, trapped and bewildered by the foreign situation, who gambled the nation's welfare on the outcome of an unrealistic scheme. He disdained all criticism, brooked no opposition, and imperiously employed the most odious means to achieve his ends. The price mattered little. Constitutional principles, public understanding, sectional interests, national treasure—all were sacrificed for the policy to which he had overcommitted himself. Refusing to consider alternatives, he believed in that policy with a passion born of desperation and a dread of war.

Jefferson also professed that an informed electorate would choose rightly when given the facts, and that it could govern wisely in the national interest if educated and involved in the process. He knew that self-government meant more than approval of the executive will by a deferential and undeliberative Congress. Yet the embargo was an expression of his will, imposed upon the nation without popular or, for that matter, congressional understanding. The way the embargo policy was formed and enforced violated the premises on which the maintenance of a free society depends.

During the embargo, the President not only did not arouse the nation; he did not give it the facts it needed nor the explanations to which it was entitled, an ironic contrast to the promise in his First Annual Address, "Nothing shall be wanting on my part to inform, as far as in my power, the legislative judgment."[2] He did not make the effort of informing the people, of seeking their understanding and cooperation, or of explaining the need for their sacrifices. He treated Congress as he treated the nation, expecting unquestioning obedience based on faith in him as President. He was accustomed to have his mere suggestion command huge majorities in a compliant Congress. While its leaders received behind-the-scenes directives, Jefferson presented an imperturbable, almost sphinxlike silence to the nation.

From his Seventh Annual Message, on October 27, 1807, which gave no hint of the impending embargo policy, to the special message on December 18, 1807, suggesting that policy, through the final embargo act of January 9, 1809, Jefferson did little to inform and educate Congress or the people. On December 17, 1807, he summoned his acquiescent cabinet and presented his draft of a message to Congress, calling for an embargo. The Secretary of Treasury had sober second thoughts. Early the next morning, he wrote to the President suggesting that an embargo "for a limited time" would be preferable to the proposed indefinite one. "In every point of view," Gallatin declared, "—privations, sufferings, revenue, effect on the enemy, politics at home, etc. —I prefer war to a permanent embargo." Government prohibitions, he observed, invariably resulted in greater "mischief" than has been anticipated, "and it is not without much hesitation that a statesman should hazard to regulate the concerns of individuals as if he could do it better than themselves." The recommendation for an embargo "being of doubtful policy and hastily adopted," Gallatin advised a time limit on the experiment.[3]

Despite Gallatin's advice, the President's message was sent to the Senate by noon of the same day. Within a few hours that deliberative body, in secret session and upon suspension of the rule requiring that a bill be read three times on three different days, passed an embargo act. A draft had probably been transmitted with the President's message. The Senate majority of over three to one steam-rolled the opposition's plea for delay and consideration.[4]

The Senate's precipitous action was based on no alarming new information from the President. He merely sent with his message a copy of the British Impressment Proclamation, news of which had already been printed in the newspapers, and notice of a French ruling that the Berlin Decree of 1806 would be enforced against neutral commerce.[5] Nor did the Senate act after a discussion of national goals by the President. He simply stated, in one hundred and seven terse words, that the dangers to American ships and seamen forced him to call Congress' attention to the fact that "advantages . . . may be expected from an inhibition of the departure from the ports of the United States."[6] In the House, the proceedings were a bit less disciplined. The bill, which mustered a two to one majority, was not passed until after three days of secret sessions.[7]

The First Embargo Act was no sooner on the books than loopholes were discovered. Coasting vessels had not been brought under the bans applicable to ocean vessels. A second embargo was therefore enacted on January 8, 1808, aimed chiefly at the trade conducted by coasting vessels with Canada and the West Indies.[8] There was no debate in the Senate and only fleeting discussion in the House, where the minority protested against the unseemly haste with which the bill was being rammed through.[9] The President shortly after sent to Congress copies of recent British orders in council, accompanied by a sixty-two-word message declaring that the enclosed documents constituted further proof that the embargo policy was justified.[10]

On March 12 the President signed into law the Third Embargo Act which, like the Second, contained further penalties, and for the first time applied to exports by land as well as by sea.[11] This measure had also been passed by Congress with no further explanation. Again there was no debate in the Senate.[12] In the House, however, Representative Barent Gardenier of New York, a Federalist, managed to get recognized and objected strenuously to the proposed bill, declaring:

> Why we passed the embargo law itself, I have been always unable to tell. Why we have passed the subsequent laws for the purpose of rendering the original evil more perfect and more universal, God only knows. It does appear to me, sir, that we are led on, step by step, but by an unseen hand . . . Darkness and mystery overshadow this House and the whole nation. We know nothing, we are permitted to know nothing. We sit here as mere automata; we legislate without knowing, nay, sir, without wishing to know, why or wherefore. We are told what we are to do, and . . . do it . . . Sir, the gentlemen of this House with whom I have the honor to act . . . are disposed to do all that men can do for their country. But we wish to know what we are doing —the tendency of the measures we are called upon to adopt. If the motives and the principles of the Administration are honest and patriotic, we would support them with a fervor which none could surpass. But, sir, we are kept in total darkness. We are treated as the enemies of our country. We are permitted to know nothing, and execrated because we do not approve of measures the origin and tendency of which are carefully concealed from us! We are denounced because we have no confidence in the Executive, at the moment the Executive refuses to discover to us—even this House, nay, sir, this nation, its actual condition.[13]

Administration supporters protested Gardenier's "slanderous" remarks and glorified the embargo policy as a great peaceable experiment in the national interest. But there was no discussion whatever of the details of the bill pending, or of the previous embargo acts, or of their constitutionality, economic impact on the nation, or infringements on personal liberty. Edward Livermore of Massachusetts then demanded a "full discussion" on the merits of the embargo policy, and Matthew Lyon of Kentucky, rising to support him, accused the majority of having acted without understanding or reason. He was ruled out of order by Speaker Macon, and the Third Embargo Act quickly thereafter passed the House by a vote of 97–22.[14]

Within a week Jefferson sent one of his rare and brief messages to Congress, this time transmitting copies of French decrees which, he said, proved the expediency of detaining American vessels, seamen, and property within their harbors until the danger passed.[15] But the President still failed to seek the nation's understanding, although resistance to the embargo had mounted to the point of systematic evasion which erupted in what the President called "insurrection." More rigorous enforcement measures originating in the White House were adopted but there was scarcely a word from Jefferson who ignored the people whom he professed to trust.

The President behaved as if he expected blind faith from his followers, although in his aloofness he called attention to the fact that Congress was responsible for the embargo policy. Statements of support from local government bodies or private organizations elicited generalized replies.[16]

His characteristic response was a gracious acknowledgment of support, coupled to a brief defense of the embargo as the only alternative to war or submission and as a means for insuring the safety of American ships and sailors. To the legislature of New Hampshire, whose coast was policed by naval gunboats and whose only important port was patrolled by revenue cutters,[17] Jefferson blithely expressed confidence that the citizens would "meet with cheerfulness the temporary privations" occasioned by the embargo.[18] His wishful thinking rested on no explanation of why the state should acquiesce in the embargo at the price of privation. In the next month New Hampshire's voters unseated the Republican majority in state offices.[19]

Jefferson's response to hostile citizens best revealed his failure to seek public understanding. Addressing himself to the citizens of the three principal port towns of New England, whose town meetings had remonstrated against embargo, he attributed their "inconveniences" to "the times in which we happen to live" and reminded them that Congress—whose New England representatives were consistently outvoted—had "passed the laws of which you complain." He thought it necessary to "advert" to the conditions that required the embargo, and once again declared it to be the only alternative to war or submission. To towns whose ships were rotting in port and whose men were unemployed, Jefferson offered the consoling thought that the embargo, "besides saving to our citizens their property, and our mariners to their country, has the peculiar advantage of giving time to the belligerent nations to revise a conduct as contrary to their interests as it is to our rights." To the request by the towns that he suspend the embargo or, failing the power to do so, convene Congress in a special session, Jefferson coolly replied that until peace was restored in Europe or the "obnoxious edicts" against American commerce were repealed, the embargo would remain in effect unless Congress prescribed a different course.[20]

The letter of the President, though not quite a high-handed dismissal of a hopelessly outvoted minority, had the wrong tone. It is not likely that anything he said, short of agreeing to work for the end of the embargo, would have satisfied his correspondents, who were as intransigent as he. But had he acknowledged the hardships resulting from the embargo on New England seaport towns, he might then have given some hint of compassion, a promise of seeking means of relief, a hope that the end might soon be in sight. He might have explained why nonintercourse and the arming of merchantmen, a policy strongly supported in New England, was in his opinion an unfeasible alternative, why, indeed, there were no feasible alternatives—for he mentioned none—to the embargo. Terse generalizations were inappropriate for the occasion at hand. A reasoned statement in defense of the embargo might not have won any votes—although many New England voters could have been won back to the Administration; but it might have cooled off enemies, encouraged friends, and suggested a willingness to debate the issue on its merits.

The Fourth Embargo Act, which Jefferson signed into law on April 25, 1808, was a drastic force act, raising special constitutional problems. They were not discussed either by the President or Congress. Of course, the constitutionality of the earlier acts, which had not been discussed, was also a major issue, because the power to regulate commerce had never been considered as an authority to prohibit it altogether. The earlier acts, however, could be defended on constitutional grounds by resorting to the loose doctrine of implied powers which Jefferson earlier had regarded as inimical to public liberty and the survival of the Union. That Jefferson, when in power, shifted his doctrine of constitutional construction is neither surprising nor worthy of criticism, although it is a little surprising that the author of the Kentucky Resolutions should have shown no concern whatever about the constitutionality of any of the embargo acts. But there was ample cause for anxiety about the Fourth Embargo Act. It carried the Administration to the precipice of unlimited and arbitrary power as measured by any American standard then known. Certainly the act mocked Republican principles by its unprecedented concentration of powers in the office of the Chief Executive, by its employment of the navy for enforcement purposes, and by its disregard of the Fourth Amendment's protections against unreasonable searches and seizures.

No ship "having any cargo aboard" could depart for any American port "or district" adjacent to foreign territory "without the special permission of the President of the United States." The navy, and revenue cutters too, on mere suspicion of an intent to evade any of the embargo laws, might anywhere stop and search any ship owned by an American citizen. The collectors of the customs, "whenever in their opinions the intention is to violate or evade" any of the embargo laws, might detain any American vessel bound for any American port, "until the decision of the President of the United States be had thereupon." Collectors might also seize deposits of any articles of "domestic growth or manufacture" adjacent to foreign territory, holding them until bond and sureties have been given for their delivery at some place in the United States. Neither warrants nor any court process were required for search and seizure.[21]

After three perfunctory readings, this bill was rushed through the Senate in a single day without debate.[22] The same tactics in the House brought Congressman Josiah Quincy to his feet, protesting that "the bill could not be understood . . . and that the operation of each section could not be distinctly seen." But the question was immediately taken on amendments intended to make the Senate bill "rigidly enforced," and after a vote of 74 to 20, the bill itself was passed on the following day without discussion.[23]

Simple respect for the electorate and for the Constitution, indeed, considerations of sheer political expediency, should have persuaded Jefferson to explain and demonstrate the need for such drastic legislation. When Americans asked in bewilderment or bitterness why they should abandon their unquestioned right to navigate the high seas or their own waterways and coastlines, or why the United States government should force a suspension of that right, even temporarily, rather than insist upon it and take appropriate measures of self-defense—arming and convoying merchant ships—they got a deaf ear from the White House. The people were being asked to submit passively, to endure, to undergo hardship, rather than fight or assert their rights. Under the circumstances, some substitute for the normal incitements to patriotic behavior was imperative. Gallatin, in explaining to the President why "a little army" would be needed to enforce the embargo, declared, "the people being distracted by the complexity of the subject, orders of council, decrees, embargoes, and wanting a single object which might rouse their patriotism and unite their passions and affections, selfishness has assumed the reins in several quarters, and the people are now there altogether against the law."[24]

Jefferson, however, spoke not at all to the nation, neither to illuminate, arouse, nor unite. To Congress he revealed little more, except in confidence to leaders like Giles or Eppes. From the time of his original note, requesting that an embargo be laid, until his Eighth Annual Message on November 8, 1808, he had three times openly communicated with Congress, each time briefly and for the purpose of transmitting foreign decrees against the rights of neutral ships and seamen. The Eighth Annual Message said scarcely more, for it contained only a short passage praising the embargo acts as a *via media* between war and surrender to foreign spoliation of American commerce.[25]

Jefferson's near silence did not signify drift, indifference, or deference to Congress. He was, all the while, exercising the boldest leadership in fashioning and enforcing embargo policies. His energy was prodigious, his direction detailed, his resolution implacable, and his spirit remorseless. The embargo acts that he neither publicly requested nor publicly explained were drafted by him or, on his orders and with his collaboration, by Secretary Gallatin.[26]

So deep was Jefferson's involvement that he personally administered certain provisions of the acts on a day-to-day basis. The President, for example, passed judgment on dozens of applications for permission to clear for a foreign port for the purpose of returning with American property. He also personally formulated the standards to guide the exercise of the detention power against suspected vessels, although he delegated to Gallatin the authority to judge individual cases appealed by collectors of the customs. His severity was suggested by the order "to consider every shipment of provisions, lumber, flaxseed, tar, cotton, tobacco, &c. enumerating the articles, as sufficiently suspicious for detention and reference here." When in doubt, he added, "consider me as voting for detention."[27]

There is no indication that he ever concerned himself with the violations of the Fourth Amendment that resulted from his policies. On one occasion, when recommending legislation to stifle the illegal trade across the Canadian border, he wanted Congress to empower his collectors to seize provisions or lumber in any port or on any coast of the United States on mere suspicion of an intent to export.[28] Gallatin redrafted the bill, at first omitting the "objectionable" provision for seizure.[29] He changed his mind, however, and recommended a very general seizure power. The power to seize property on land, without warrant, after being approved by the House was finally restricted by the Senate to areas adjacent to foreign territory, but collectors were not even required to suspect an intent to evade the embargo.[30]

As civil disobedience spread, Jefferson's resolution stiffened; he yielded increasingly to the temptation to employ any means, however draconian, to force compliance. The embargo, begun as a means of coercing and starving England and France into respect for American rights, rapidly became an instrument of coercion against American citizens. To avoid foreign war, Jefferson made domestic war. He fought some of his own people, who believed that the national government had no right to deprive them of their ability to earn a livelihood or to conduct an inquisition into their business affairs. They believed, too, that the Constitution protected their right to trade and insured them against any equivalent of the despised writs of assistance that had been used by the British before the Revolution.

Popular resistance simply enraged the President, whose executive temper remained at the flash point. He even considered starving out American communities to break their spirit. The embargo was supposed to starve European nations. But Jefferson did not hesitate to refuse a permit that was requested to allow a schooner to carry provisions and lumber to a town at the mouth of the Penobscot River in Maine. "This," he reported to the Secretary of the Treasury, "is the first time the character of the place has been brought under consideration as an objection." A general disobedience in any particular place, he explained, must be considered in deciding to refuse a permit or any other means that might contribute to that disobedience. "In such a case we may fairly require positive proof that the individual of a town tainted with a general spirit of disobedience, has never said or done anything himself to countenance that spirit. But the first cause of refusal being sufficient, an inquiry into character and conduct is unnecessary."[31] Thus, Jefferson inclined to attaint and blockade a whole locality, because some of its citizens dared to speak against his embargo policies and one may have said or done something to warrant a suspicion of intent to evade.

Jefferson was ready to apply his principle of guilt by association to the island of Nantucket, off the Massachusetts mainland, upon receiving a petition for a shipment of food. "Our opinion here," wrote the President to the governor of Massachusetts, "is that that place has been so deeply concerned in smuggling, that if it wants [for food], it is because it has illegally sent away what it ought to have retained for its own consumption."[32] Happily this harsh opinion was put in the form of a recommendation, rather than an order. Community proscription was more a wish than a practice, but the President's suppressive temper was clear enough.

To resist him, even to say anything countenancing a spirit of disobedience, was the mark of an enemy to be overcome by naked power. On April 19, 1808, the anniversary of the first battle of the American Revolution, the President issued a proclamation declaring the existence of an insurrection "too powerful to be suppressed by the ordinary course of judicial proceedings" in the region of Lake Champlain, where giant rafts ferried foodstuffs into Canada from Vermont and New York. All persons having authority, civil or military, and "all other persons, civil or military, who shall be found within the vicinage," were ordered "by all means in their power, by force of arms or otherwise" to aid in the suppression of the insurrection.[33] The governors of New York and Vermont ordered out militia detachments, too late, however, to capture the raftsmen.

The townspeople of Saint Albans, Vermont, responded by a memorial to the President, protesting against his proclamation as unwarranted. If, they declared, a few individuals had evaded the embargo restrictions, "this could never furnish a just cause for proclaiming to the world that insurrection and rebellion were chargeable on the good people of this district."[34]

They did not know and therefore could not remind Jefferson that he had once philosophically observed, "And what country can preserve it's [*sic*] liberties if their rulers are not warned from time to time that their people preserve the spirit of resistance? Let them take arms. The remedy is to set them right as to facts, pardon and pacify them . . . The tree of liberty must be refreshed from time to time with the blood of patriots and tyrants. It is it's [*sic*] natural manure."[35] It was in this reflective mood of halcyon days that he had lightly dismissed the alarm provoked by Shay's Rebellion and expressed concern if America should long be without an insurrection. No amount of power in the government, he had written, could prevent insurrections. Domestic peace, he had believed, was best preserved not by giving energy to the government but by giving "information to the people . . . Educate and inform the whole mass of the people. Enable them to see that it is their interest to preserve peace and order, and they will preserve them."[36] The responsibilities of the office of the presidency during a time of crisis apparently had given him new insights: keep the people in the dark, use armed force against them, and they will see the error of their ways.

The proclamation of insurrection had been based on the authority of the President to suppress insurrections, dating back to a statute of 1792 that authorized the calling out of the state militia whenever the laws of the United States were opposed or their execution obstructed by combinations too powerful to be suppressed by the ordinary course of judicial proceedings or by the power vested in the federal marshals. Under this early statute, which Washington had used to crush the

Whiskey Rebellion of 1794, the President could call forth the militia only after being notified by a federal judge that military force was necessary and after first issuing a proclamation commanding the insurgents to disperse. By a revision of 1795, judicial determination of the necessity of military intervention was abolished, and the President was made "exclusive judge" of the facts warranting his calling on the militia. The statute also authorized him to resort to military measures in cases of "domestic violence."[37] Upon this statute Adams based his authority to suppress Fries' Rebellion.

During the administrations of Federalist presidents, no act was passed authorizing the use of the regular army or navy to put down domestic violence. That step was not taken by the government until Jefferson's presidency, although he had previously been a militant enemy of the army, a champion of the local militias, and had bitterly opposed the use of even the militia against Pennsylvania farmers during the Whiskey Rebellion and Fries' Rebellion. But after Burr's conspiracy, it was believed that the militia, which Jefferson in his First Inaugural Address had called "our best reliance," might not be able to cope with certain "insurrections." Consequently an act of 1807 authorized the President to use "the land or naval force of the United States" in any case where it would be lawful for him to call out the militia, provided that he "first observed all the prerequisites of the law in that respect."[38] As of April 1808, Jefferson did not yet dare use the regular army to suppress "insurrections" against the embargo. That step was soon to be taken, however.

The army had historically been the Republican bête noire. Jefferson himself had long been the principal spokesman in the nation on the inevitable tyranny that resulted from maintaining "standing" armies in time of peace. When the Federalists raised twelve regiments in 1798, after hundreds of American ships had been sunk or captured by the French and when a two-year undeclared naval war was beginning, the Jeffersonians wailed that the troops would destroy liberty at home.

At the conclusion of the crisis with France, the Federalists reduced the army to 5000 men, and Jefferson, on becoming President, reduced it still further to 3000. The surplus men, he argued, were not needed for garrison duty; for defense against invasion "their number is as nothing; nor is it conceived needful or safe that a standing army should be kept up in time of peace for that purpose."[39] In his Sixth Annual Message, delivered December 2, 1806, only one week after a proclamation warning the populace of a dangerous military enterprise in the West—Burr's conspiracy—and when war with Spain seemed imminent enough to justify a call for five hundred volunteer cavalry and the reinforcement of our border garrisons, Jefferson declared: "Were armies to be raised whenever a speck of war is visible in our horizon, we never should have been without them." Until war broke out, he assured, the militia was adequate for defense of the nation.[40]

When, therefore, in January 1808, Representative George W. Campbell of Tennessee moved consideration of a Senate bill that would increase the army by one battalion of riflemen, one of cavalry, and one regiment of infantry, it was not surprising that Speaker Macon should rise to argue that he did not believe it necessary to "make so large an addition to our present Peace Establishment."[41] It was not surprising either that Representative John W. Eppes, the President's son-in-law, should also oppose the bill with great vigor. Recalling the "tyranny" of 1798, Eppes discoursed on the old theme of the incompatibility of liberty and standing armies. Was it not true, he demanded, that the army would be used to "overawe sedition" once again? "Oppression and tyranny," Eppes warned, "will drive the people to rebellion, and standing armies produce both." In great heat he added, "I never yet have voted for a regular army or soldier in time of peace. Whenever an opportunity has offered, I have voted them down, and, so help me God, I will as long as I live."[42]

Shortly thereafter, Eppes rose on the floor of the House to explain why he would vote to increase the regular army by 6000 men! The reason for his somersault was patent. Ten days after he vowed eternal opposition against standing armies in time of peace, President Jefferson startled Congress with a message declaring that the dangerous state of foreign affairs required the augmentation of the regular army. Accompanying the characteristically brief presidential message, which failed to explain why the foreign situation had suddenly become so dangerous, was a statement from the Secretary of War, Henry Dearborn, proposing an addition of eight regiments or 6000 men.[43]

The congressional Republicans, although caught unaware by this stunning blow to their cherished doctrines against standing armies, recovered with great agility. Although the army was to be raised for five years in time of peace, they quickly convinced themselves that considerations of national security fully justified their abrupt reversal of position. But some of the Feds and Quids jeeringly raked the administration with reminders of the past. Their argument against the measure was incisive as well as embarrassing. They condemned a standing army in time of peace as inconsistent with the embargo policy which was supposed to save all the expense and danger of armies. The proposed army, they pointed out, was only large enough to compel compliance with the embargo laws at the point of a bayonet and at the price of freedom, but was too ridiculously small to be a defense against invasion.[44] The measure passed the House by a vote of 95 to 16.[45] Events proved that the minority's forensic parade of imaginary horribles was justified: the army would be used to enforce the embargo laws.

The expansion of the regular army by no means signified that Republican reliance on the militia had been abandoned. Jefferson had determined on a program of national preparedness in case the embargo failed to bring England and France to heel. Nearly two million dollars was appropriated for gunboats and land fortifications, and another million for a vastly expanded militia under an act of March 30, 1808. That act authorized the President to require the governors to organize, arm, equip, "and hold in readiness to march at a moment's warning" 100,000 militiamen. The act also provided that the President be empowered "to call into actual service any part, or the whole" of the 100,000 men "when he shall judge that the exigencies of the United States require it."[46] This was a remarkable delegation of authority to the President for a period of two years, given the fact that the Constitution precisely states that *Congress* may provide "for calling forth the Militia to execute the Laws of the Union, suppress Insurrections and repel Invasions." Thus the act delegating so broad a grant of authority to the President without specifying standards to guide his judgment, was of dubious constitutionality; but in 1808, when unprecedented powers were almost daily being concentrated in and exercised by the office of the Executive, constitutional proprieties were not permitted to interfere with vigorous leadership.

The navy was called into active duty in enforcing the embargo policy even before the militia. The First Embargo Act specified that "the President be authorized to give such instructions to the officers of the revenue and of the navy and revenue cutters . . . as shall appear best adapted for carrying the same into full effect."[47] Two days later, Jefferson had spotted deficiencies in the act, prodded Gallatin to suggest amendments, and ordered that "In the meantime the revenue cutters and armed vessels must use force."[48]

The First Embargo Act, however, authorized the use of the navy only against ships bound for foreign ports without presidential clearance. The Second Embargo Act, which was aimed against vessels engaged in the coastal trade, contained no provision for naval enforcement. Jefferson operated in a twilight zone of authority, therefore, when he ordered the Secretary of the Navy, Robert Smith, to send gunboats to intercept American ships trading with British ships off the Delaware coast.[49] In his draft of the Fourth Embargo Act, Jefferson provided for "the armed vessels of the United States to bring to and examine all vessels suspected" of intending or attempting to evade the embargo laws.[50] Section seven of the Act, as passed, contained the needed authority for the navy to search any American vessels on mere suspicion wherever they might be found on the high seas, the coastal waters, the inland waterways, or in any port. When the insurrection broke out on Lake Champlain, the militia was backed up by gunboats which were sent to patrol the water boundary line.

By July 1808 the navy was regularly used to enforce the embargo. Jefferson instructed the Secretary of the Navy to place his forces at the disposal of Gallatin, the chief enforcement officer for the embargo. The President declared: "Complaints multiply upon us of evasions of the embargo laws, by fraud and force . . . As I do consider the severe enforcement of the embargo to be of an importance, not to be measured by money, for our future government, as well as present objects, I think it will be advisable that during this summer all the gunboats, actually manned and commissioned, should be distributed through as many ports and bays as may be necessary to assist the embargo."[51] Thus, the navy, which had first been used in emergencies only, soon became an instrument of routine enforcement. It was a new departure in American history to send the navy into action, on a daily basis, not against a foreign enemy, but against American citizens.

The expanded regular army was ordered to enforce the embargo laws by the summer of 1808. As early as May 28 Gallatin had recommended sending "a company of regulars" to the disaffected area in the Lake Champlain area, where the militia had, without much success, been called out to throttle the constant smuggling of provisions across the Canadian boundary.[52] By July, after Jefferson had received constant complaints of "the breach of embargo by fraud and force on our northern water line," he instructed the Secretary of War, General

Dearborn, to cooperate with Gallatin "by rendezvousing as many new recruits as you can in that quarter."[53]

The situation on the northern boundary, particularly in the lakes region, was extremely critical. There were numerous incidents of smuggling, some accompanied by violence, even pitched battles with the militia. In one engagement, thirty-nine men were said to have been wounded. In another, on July 2, a detachment of soldiers was overpowered by a gang seeking, successfully, to recapture some potash that had been seized in an earlier smuggling attempt.[54] The act of 1807, passed in the aftermath of the Burr conspiracy, authorized the President to call forth the armed forces of the United States in any case in which the militia might lawfully be called, namely, whenever in the opinion of the President there existed domestic violence or obstruction to the execution of the laws by combinations too powerful to be suppressed by the federal marshals.

Jefferson used his power liberally, although it is not at all clear that he obeyed the requirements of the act of 1807 which obligated him to comply with "all the prerequisites of the law" before calling any troops, whether militiamen or regulars. One of the prerequisites of the law required him to proclaim publicly the existence of a condition justifying the employment of the armed forces and commanding the "insurgents" to disperse. Jefferson never again issued such a proclamation after that of April 19, 1808, probably because it had provoked considerable criticism. He may have acted under the novel theory that the proclamation of that date, which applied to "Lake Champlain, and . . . the country thereto adjacent," was permanently in effect for that region, for the troops stayed there. That theory, however farfetched, could justify the continuing use of the armed forces in that region only. It could not warrant the use of troops elsewhere in the absence of a proclamation. It could not, for example, clothe with legality Jefferson's instruction to General Dearborn to "fly" to the scene of a threatened insurrection by the "tories of Boston," who were resisting the Administration's efforts to close the interstate importation of flour, and "on the first symptom of an open opposition of the law by force" to "aid in suppressing any commotion."[55] On the same day, the President informed his Secretary of the Navy that the Secretary of War had been requested "to be on the alert, and fly to the spot where any open and forcible opposition shall be commenced, and to crush it in embryo."[56]

The outbreak at Boston did not materialize, but trouble occurred at Oswego, New York, revealing Jefferson's reluctance to issue any public proclamation. On August 9, Gallatin transmitted a letter from Governor Tompkins of New York announcing an "insurrection." The Secretary of the Treasury presumed the accounts to be exaggerated, and declared that "there is no more insurrection than has been on Lake Champlain"[57]—an astonishing statement, given the President's proclamation of April 19 that an insurrection did exist there, and given, too, the fact that troops, including regulars, had been constantly stationed in the areas of disaffection on the Vermont side.

As for the situation at Oswego, insurrection or not, it justified in Gallatin's mind the calling of the militia. "I had a long conference with the governor," he reported to the President, "and stated your reluctance to issue another proclamation declaring a part of this State in a state of insurrection. He felt the force of the observation, and declared his willingness to do whatever he could *legally and properly* do." Gallatin on his own authority had assured Tompkins that if he called out the militia, the expense would be paid by the United States. "I think that it will be necessary that you should give him assurances to the same effect." Five hundred men would be enough, thought Gallatin, and he presented the President with a plan for deploying the troops. He also warned that because of General Dearborn's negligence, "we have not one man besides the regulars in readiness."[58]

As a matter of fact, Tompkins did not at all think an insurrection existed. His letter to Jefferson, enclosed with Gallatin's, alleged that the customs collector had overstated the situation in order to secure militia aid which the governor thought not justified.[59] The President, from Monticello, hastened to assure the governor of New York that the opposition to the embargo in New York "being arrayed in a war-like manner, actually committing acts of war . . . brings it so fully within the legal definition of an insurrection, that I should not hesitate to issue a proclamation, were I not restrained by motives of which your Excellency seems to be apprised." Urging Tompkins to "render a great public service," Jefferson promised to pay the bill for not more than five hundred men.[60] A copy of the correspondence with Tompkins went to Gallatin, whose next letter assured the President that the "opposition at Oswego has broken into insurrection."[61] Tompkins, he reported, had agreed to call out "one or two companies of militia."[62]

But Tompkins had not agreed and was extremely reluctant to pull the President's chestnuts out of the fire. He answered the President's letter by urging court action before attempting force. The way to proceed, he argued, was for the President to send "some competent legal character" to those places where the embargo laws had been most frequently violated, and gather evidence "to convict the offenders in the Courts of the United States. I am persuaded a few prosecutions and convictions would have a greater tendency to make the laws respected than the appearance of a Military force."[63] Jefferson, however, probably remembered Gallatin's report of a month earlier that in Vermont, "a Republican jury," despite the efforts of the prosecuting attorney and the support given to him by the charge of the judge, had refused to find bills against prisoners who had been captured in the act of violating the embargo.[64] Jefferson persisted, and Tompkins finally bowed to his will.

Under cover of Tompkins' calling forth of the militia, the administration was in a position to justify, at least in part, dispatching detachments of the regular army to the Lake Ontario region. Gallatin, as early as August 19, had requested the President to "direct General Wilkinson to order immediately all the recruits in the State of New York, including those in the city, to repair, about 1/3 to Sacket's Harbor, on Lake Ontario; 1/3 to Oswegatchie, on St. Lawrence; and 1/3 to Plattsburg, on Lake Champlain" to enforce the embargo laws.[65] The President followed this recommendation precisely.[66] But he issued no proclamation of his own, contrary to the law which directed the use of the regular army. He acted strongly, swiftly, silently, and semilegally, avoiding the public disfavor and contemptuous reaction which had met his public proclamation of April.

Clearly Jefferson had no authority whatever, without issuing a proclamation, to send troops to the Saint Lawrence River. It is equally clear that he had little faith, after all, in the militia. Experience showed, he explained to General Wilkinson, that the militia on the Canadian border had proved to be "expensive, troublesome, and less efficacious."[67] What he meant was that the local militia too often cooperated with embargo violations or winked at them. Wilkinson was instructed to relieve the militia throughout New York. By mid-September, Gallatin was able to report, "I hope that by the 1st of October everything will be there (on the Lakes) in tolerable order, and the militia relieved everywhere but in Vermont by the regulars."[68] Thus by late summer of 1808, the regular army, the previously dreaded "standing army in time of peace," was regularly employed in the enforcement of the embargo laws in the Northeastern United States. By the same time, naval gunboats and revenue cutters patrolled the inland waterways and coasts of the nation.

On a prolonged, widespread, and systematic basis, in some places lasting nearly a year, the armed forces harried and beleaguered the citizenry. Never before or since did American history exhibit such a spectacle of derangement of normal values and perspectives. On the two earlier occasions when the national government crushed insurrections, the areas of disaffection were localized, the insurgents were speedily overcome, the army was immediately withdrawn, and civil authority was promptly restored. Under Jefferson, from the summer of

1808 until the time he left office, in March of 1809, "insurrections" were continuous throughout an entire section of the nation and the armed forces were employed on a sustained basis, as if it were normal for American soldiers and sailors to enforce against American citizens their own laws.

The President, profoundly pacifistic, had answered foreign attacks on American commerce by a steady siege against American commerce and by quartering troops among the American people. The result, in Henry Adams' words, was that, "Personal liberties and rights of property were more directly curtailed in the United States by embargo than in Great Britain by centuries of almost continuous foreign war."[69] Substantial segments of the people genuinely believed that their government was at war with them. Their government, in turn, believed that a powerful minority, operating from Saint Marys, Georgia, to Passamaquoddy, Maine, was engaged in a continuous and defiant sabotage, verging sometimes on war against the government, at all times jeopardizing national security.

Jefferson himself, as the situation steadily worsened, came to believe that the opposition to his policy, when of a forcible nature, was treasonable. It is revealing that when he sought to convince Governor Tompkins that the Oswego situation met the "legal definition of insurrection," he used language meeting the Constitution's definition of treason: "arrayed in a war-like manner, actually committing acts of war." From his language, from his temper at the time—as revealed in his correspondence—and from subsequent events, it is a fair inference that he meant to employ any means, including prosecutions for treason, to enforce the embargo.

✧ Chapter Six ✧

Any Means to the End: The Embargo, II

AN EXCHANGE of summer letters between President Jefferson and Secretary of the Treasury Gallatin disclosed the disorder of the American political system during 1808. Had James Madison, the Secretary of State and "father" of the Bill of Rights, been a party to the opinions expressed on this occasion, a rival to Alice's Wonderland would have been created to distract Clio's sanity. Jefferson and Gallatin, two of the three titans in the history of American libertarianism, confronted a major crisis that shook the democratic character of the Administration; and they responded by considering ways and means of assaulting liberty in a manner that matched the repressive imaginations of the Essex Junto.

In twelve hundred words of steely realism,[1] the Secretary of the Treasury briefed the President on the most pressing question of the time: what to do about the embargo? The picture, as of July 29, was bleak. Violations steadily mounted. Although the situation off the Delaware, the Chesapeake, and North Carolina was alarming, the greatest dangers existed from New York to Passamaquoddy and the Canadian border. Four enactments, the last of which was the enforcement act of

April, had been inadequate. Congress had failed to give collectors sufficient power to seize any articles suspected of being destined for shipment in violation of the laws. Seizures could be made only off the coast or at points adjacent to foreign territory. What was needed, urged Gallatin, was the adoption of his suggestion (originally Jefferson's) that the seizure power be made "general." Few collectors would seize property, however suspicious, without lawful authorization. One with "nerve and zeal" had made "several doubtful seizures, for which he is sued." Others could not be expected to "risk all they are worth in doubtful cases; and it results that, until Congress meets [in November], we must depend entirely on force for checking this manner of violating the law." All the gunboats, cruisers, and cutters that could be spared had been ordered "northwardly." The situation "on the Lakes," particularly at Ontario and Champlain, was "no better." "Nothing but force on *land* (for there the collectors have the right to seize property on shore) will put a stop to the violations." Little could be expected by way of judicial redress.

There were only two possible courses of action, Gallatin advised: prepare for war or make the embargo work.

> I am perfectly satisfied that if the embargo must be persisted in any longer, two principles must necessarily be adopted in order to make it sufficient: 1st, that not a single vessel shall be permitted to move without the special permission of the Executive; 2d, that the collectors be invested with the general power of seizing property anywhere, and taking the rudders or otherwise effectually preventing the departure of any vessel in harbor, though ostensibly intended to remain there; and that without being liable to personal suits. I am sensible that such arbitrary powers are

equally dangerous and odious. But a restrictive measure of the nature of the embargo applied to a nation under such circumstances as the United States cannot be enforced without the assistance of means as strong as the measure itself. To that legal authority to prevent, seize, and detain must be added a sufficient physical force to carry it into effect; and although I believe that in our seaports little difficulty would be encountered, we must have a little army along the Lakes and British lines generally.[2]

Having stressed that "arbitrary" powers, both "dangerous and odious," were necessary for the embargo's success, Gallatin once again pointed out its unpopularity and its systematic evasion. The same thing, he added, had occurred in Europe, "even under the strongest governments under similar circumstances." The British navy had not prevented smuggling, and "you recollect, doubtless, the army of *employés* and the sanguinary code of France,—hardly adequate to guard their land frontiers [against illegal trading]."

Gallatin's letter concluded with a statement of his own incapacity to decide which horn of the dilemma to be impaled against. Failure of the embargo meant "we must submit and prepare for war." Retaining the embargo meant "that Congress must . . . invest the Executive with the most arbitrary powers and sufficient force to carry the embargo into effect." If the embargo were surrendered to avoid arbitrary government, "I see no alternative but war. But with whom?" That plaintive question implied the insanity of challenging simultaneously the world's great sea and land powers, and the impossibility of deciding to challenge one rather than the other, when both were equally guilty. The question, ended Gallatin, should be decided "on the ground of justice." The President alone, knowing the probable results one way or the other, must make the decision.

Jefferson, who two months later expressed the opinion that in extreme cases "the universal resource is a dictator,"[3] replied decisively. He showed, as Henry Adams observed, no offense that a member of his cabinet should suggest the adoption of "the most arbitrary powers."[4] The prospect of resorting to means "equally dangerous and odious" was not repellent. His answer betrayed neither a shade of doubt nor a sense of the tragedy that hovered over his decision. "Congress," he tersely instructed, "must legalize all *means* which may be necessary to obtain its *end*."[5] What Congress did would be largely prescribed by the President, with the assistance of Gallatin.

Gallatin's letter and Jefferson's response revealed the colossal failure of statesmanship that afflicted the Administration. Neither one discussed the possibility of searching for means to alleviate the hardships resulting from the embargo. Neither saw any alternative other than war or measures of an arbitrary and military nature for enforcement against the American people. Neither considered the possibility of nonintercourse with Great Britain and France, a strong naval program (Jefferson built gunboats to enforce the embargo, but not a single frigate), the arming of merchant ships and protecting them with convoys, a vigorous program of public education, and perhaps the issuance of letters of marque and reprisal against France and England.

The President, shortly after accepting the doctrine that the ends justified the means, ordered out the regular army as a normal enforcement agency, without the formality of public proclamation, and without lawful authority. He permitted his Attorney General to experiment with a treason prosecution as another means of enforcement. He deliberately and lawlessly ordered collectors of the customs, to ignore a decision by a Supreme Court justice who ruled that the President had acted without statutory authority. He recommended a new enforcement act that subverted the Bill of Rights and possessed little semblance of constitutionality. The gentle, libertarian philosopher, who never forgot the painful criticism that he had been a timid and indecisive war governor of Virginia, had become a presidential autocrat.

Jefferson certainly did not conceive of himself as above the law and he was hardly a Bonaparte. Yet he stretched the law to a breaking point. Largely dependent upon Congress, however, for delegation of the powers he wanted, he was sometimes disappointed in a way that a Bonaparte would never have been. Napoleon, for example, would have summarily destroyed any vessels that stood in his way. Jefferson, finding embargo violations at Saint Marys, Georgia, "embarrassing," was reduced to asking Gallatin's opinion "how it might do to destroy all boats and canoes on our side of the river, paying for them?"[6] He had slight choice but to abide by the answer: "We cannot destroy the boats, &c., at St. Mary's without being authorized by law so to do; and Congress shows so much reluctance in granting powers much less arbitrary, that there is no expectation of their giving this."[7] The suggestion by the President was nevertheless a remarkable example of the extreme measures he was prepared to adopt.

The same tone appeared in Jefferson's relations with the federal judiciary in 1808. His intense hostility to the courts, dominated by Federalists, had more often than not been well founded. The independence of the federal judiciary seemed to Jefferson a mere guise for political judgments. The failure of the government to obtain a single conviction in any of the Burr conspiracy prosecutions in 1807 left the President in no mood for judicial interposition that would snag the enforcement of the embargo. To his embarrassment, it was a judge of his own appointment and party, William Johnson of the Supreme Court, who thwarted him. To make matters worse, it was a resolutely Federalist judge, John Davis of the United States District Court of Massachusetts, of all places, who unexpectedly sustained the Administration; while another Republican jurist appointed by the President, Brockholst Livingston, struck with one of the most scathing opinions ever aimed at the government. The year 1808 was certainly a bad one in Jefferson's relations with the judiciary.

Justice Johnson's opinion, that the President had exceeded his statutory authority, turned on the detention power. In the Fourth Embargo Act, initially drafted by the President himself, collectors of the customs were empowered to detain any vessel "ostensibly bound with a cargo to some other port of the United States, whenever in their opinions the intention is to violate or evade" any of the provisions of the embargo laws, until the decision of the President can be had.[8] The discretion to detain was therefore vested by Congress in the collectors. The President might approve or disapprove of a collector's decision to detain, but he was not authorized to pass judgment in any case in which a collector gave clearance. Jefferson preferred to read the statute as if it vested the discretionary power in him. Congress, he wrote Gallatin, "finally gave us the power of detention as the panacea, and I am clear we ought to use it freely."[9] He laid down broad standards for the guidance of collectors, binding them to refuse clearance in all cases of doubt or whenever the cargo was "suspicious," which is to say, whenever it was cotton, foodstuffs, or any materials in demand in European markets. Gallatin, complying with the President's directive, issued appropriate instructions to the collectors of the customs, thereby foreclosing their discretion in the vast majority of cases.[10]

In compliance with a Treasury Department circular, expressing the wishes of the President, Simeon Theus, collector of the Port of Charleston, refused clearance for a ship bound from Charleston to Baltimore with a cargo of cotton and rice. The facts of the case showed why Jefferson's excessively rigorous enforcement alienated public support. The shipowners, apprehensive that the *Resource* might rot in port, advertised to carry freight to Baltimore. They contracted to carry six hundred bales of cotton and, in addition, two hundred barrels of rice, freight free, as ballast. The cargo had been loaded under inspection of a revenue officer; all requirements of the laws had been complied with—and Theus denied clearance. The indignant owners immediately sought relief from the United States Circuit Court in Charleston, Justice Johnson presiding. They sued for a writ of mandamus commanding the collector to give clearance, as he affirmed he would have were it not for instructions from Washington. Theus, in his response to the court's order to show cause why the mandamus should not be issued, admitted that he had no suspicion of an intention by the owners to violate the embargo laws, but declared that he was bound by executive orders to deny clearance.[11]

The question, stated Justice Johnson, was whether the "instructions of the President through the Secretary of the Treasury, unsupported by an act of Congress, will justify the collector in that detention." There was "no doubt" of the answer. "The officers of our government, from the highest to the lowest, are equally subjected to legal restraint; and it is confidently believed that all of them feel themselves equally incapable, as well from law as from inclination, to attempt an unsanctioned encroachment upon individual liberty." Having tactfully but firmly announced that the President was not above the rule of law, Johnson ruled that the discretionary right to grant clearance had been clearly vested in the collector, not the executive, who therefore could not bind the collector's judgment.[12]

The sensational publicity given to Johnson's opinion by the Federalist press damaged the President. Because of his illegal conduct, Jefferson was pitilessly assaulted for executive usurpations at the expense of "individual liberty," in Johnson's phrase; and much was made of the unassailable fact that the judicial rebuke could not be dismissed as partisan politics.[13] When Jefferson received a copy of the proceedings, he responded by declaring his "great concern" because the opinion of a Republican judge of his own appointment from a Republican state "could not be ascribed to any political waywardness." His instructions to the collectors, he explained, had been founded on a desire to establish a uniform administration of the embargo act, in the interest of fairness and efficiency. The question decided by Johnson "has too many important bearings on the constitutional organization of our government, to let it go off so carelessly." He had therefore obtained an opinion on the question from his attorney general which, he said, was being "communicated to the collectors and marshals for their future government."[14] Thus Jefferson determined to overrule the federal court.

The opinion of Attorney General Caesar Rodney, superseding that of Justice Johnson, sustained the President in every respect, of course. But the bulk of Rodney's opinion was an attack on the judge for interfering with the executive by issuing a madamus not within the jurisdiction of his court.[15] When Rodney's opinion was released to the press as the law applicable for the guidance of collectors in all future cases, the President was deservedly accused of contempt for constitutional government. His overgenerous interpretation of his power to control collectors' discretion to detain was excusable; his repudiation and overruling of a federal judge was not. Does the President, asked the Charleston *Courier,* mean to dominate the judiciary "in terrorem?" It was an attempt "the like of which has never been witnessed by the citizens of the United States who have been accustomed to regard in reverence the solemn decisions of the highest tribunals," to secure "subservience" to the Chief Executive, declared a Philadelphia newspaper. "Well may we consider our liberties as in danger."[16]

Justice Johnson, stung by Rodney's criticism, resorted to the press in his own defense. Exalting the supremacy of the Constitution and the rule of law, he warned that exemption of the President from accountability before the courts might establish a precedent "which in the hands of an unprincipled and intrepid president (and we may have the misfortune to see such a one elevated to that post)" would have evil effects. The attorney general's argument on the want of jurisdiction in the court to issue a mandamus, he pointed out, "will not prove the legality of the instructions given to the collector. The argument [by Rodney] is not that the Executive have done right, but that the Judiciary had no power to prevent their doing wrong."[17] Jefferson's conduct deserved Justice Johnson's condemnation.

The President's next encounter with the federal judiciary was less personal but far more punishing. In June of 1808, an incident, during the continuous "insurrection" in the Lake Champlain area of Vermont, led to an experiment in embargo enforcement and a judicial condemnation to which the Administration dared not call attention. A militia company, stationed at Alburg, Vermont, had captured a large raft loaded with lumber and illegally headed for the nearby Canadian market. The soldiers had run it aground a short distance away from their camp, and a guard of a dozen men was left to watch it at night. The owner of the raft hired some sixty lumberjacks to rescue his raft from the military, promising them $800 for their night's work. Ten or twelve of the rescuers, including one Frederick Hoxie, were armed with muskets, the rest with clubs and spiked poles. They managed to get the raft afloat before the guards finally aroused and gave the alarm, turning out the camp. As the raft floated slowly northward, shots were exchanged until the smugglers were out of sight and safely on the way to Canada. No one was injured.[18]

Incidents of this kind were too numerous to overlook. In the following month a gang of Vermonters recaptured from the military a supply of confiscated potash. In August two soldiers were killed in a clash with armed smugglers near Rutland.[19] Similar incidents occurred elsewhere on the northern border. Thwarted and angry, the President called Gallatin's attention to "what is passing on the Canada line. To prevent it is, I suppose, beyond our means, but we must try to harass the unprincipled agents, and punish as many as we can."[20] The offenders, he said, referring to one incident, must be made to feel the consequences of daring to oppose a law by force.[21]

As a result the government made a test case out of the incident at Alburg involving Frederick Hoxie and five others who had rescued the raft of lumber in June. Collector Jabez Penniman filed a complaint for the arrest of the men, and at the direction of Attorney General Rodney they were charged with treason.[22] "Penniman's conduct," observed Jefferson, "deserves marked approbation, and there should be no hesitation about the expenses reasonably incurred. If all these people are convicted, there will be too many to be punished with death. My hope is that they will send me full statements of every man's case, that the most guilty may be marked as examples, and the less so suffer long imprisonment under reprieves from time to time."[23]

The trial for treason was held October 27, 1808, in the United States Circuit Court at Burlington, Justice Brockholst Livingston of New York, who had been appointed to the Supreme Court by the President in 1807, presiding. Charging the jury on the law of treason, Livingston emphasized that the crime, in time of peace, could consist only of levying war against the United

States. The framers of the Constitution, he declared, in order to prevent "every abuse by the extension of treason to offenses, which in times of public agitation, might, by violent or corrupt constructions, be pretended to belong to it," had carefully defined the crime by "a rule which was to be binding on every department of government." An offense less than the actual levying of war, however atrocious, was not treason, though punishable if made criminal by congressional enactment. In this case, despite the "artificial dress" of the indictment, there was "nothing more" than the forcible rescue of a raft from the custody of the military guard placed over it by the collector.

> It is impossible to suppress the astonishment which is excited at the attempt which has been made to convince a court and jury of this high criminal jurisdiction, that, between this and the levying of war, there is no difference. Can it be seriously thought that an American jury, with the constitution of the United States as a guide to their interpretation, or even on the cases which have been cited, can be brought by engrafting construction on construction, to leave far behind them, English judges and English juries, in their exposition of the crime of treason?[24]

The case, continued Justice Livingston, showed not war against the United States but an opposition to the law that was transitory, "free from every traitorous intention," and conducted for the sole purpose of private gain. The prisoners, having been paid, returned peaceably and quietly to their homes, "not suspecting that they had a war on their hands, with any power, and least of all with the government of their own country." Between the present case and that of the insurrectionists of 1794 and 1798, relied upon by the government as precedents, there was a great difference.[25] There was also a distinction between treason on the one hand and on the other, conspiracy, trespass, riot, larceny, and assault and battery. The court, concluded Livingston, would not establish a "precedent so dangerous, or one that will in any degree tend to demolish that barrier which has been raised by the constitution against constructive treason." The jury, reported a Burlington newspaper laconically, "in a few minutes" returned a verdict of not guilty.[26]

Jefferson's only allusion to this case was a remark that the opposition to the embargo "in one quarter amounted almost to rebellion and treason."[27] After the lashing from an unimpeachably Republican member of the Supreme Court, whose outrage contrasted so vividly with the temperate remarks of Chief Justice Marshall in the Burr case, the affair was best forgotten. The result not only blocked another effort by the President to insinuate dread doctrines of constructive treason in American constitutional law; it ended any further attempt to enforce the embargo against "forcible offenders" by treason prosecutions.

Jefferson's only solace in his relations with the federal judiciary during the period of the embargo was tinged with gall, for the sole victory won by the Administration, and a major one at that, was due to a judge from the enemy camp. Judge John Davis, a lifelong Massachusetts Federalist, sitting in Salem, the heart of the Essex Junto, sustained the constitutionality of the embargo laws in an opinion of sweeping nationalism. The case raised the question whether Congress could prohibit commerce in the exercise of its power to regulate it. Questions involving unreasonable search and seizure were not at issue.

Davis' decision[28] was founded on a broad reading of the commerce power and the "inherent sovereignty" of the United States—a construction of the Constitution that Jefferson, before becoming President, had condemned as irreconcilable with civil liberty. Davis' demonstration of the independence of the federal judiciary made Jefferson's repeated assaults on the partisanship of the bench look foolish, especially when measured against the courage of the judge to resist enormous pressures on him to decide in favor of local interests and opinion.[29] The final irony of the case was that the principal lawyer for the government, George Blake, United States district attorney for Massachusetts, had been the subject of Gallatin's criticism to the President for "laxity" in prosecuting embargo cases.[30] When a vacancy later occurred on the Supreme Court, Jefferson read Blake out of the party, although he had won the most important case of all and was an outstanding libertarian theorist and lawyer.[31] Writing to Madison, Jefferson declared, "Blake calls himself republican, but never was one at heart. His treachery to us under the embargo should put him by forever."[32]

Shortly after Judge Davis sustained the constitutionality of the embargo, Jefferson, mindful that Congress would soon reconvene, took steps to fulfill his promise that all means necessary for the successful enforcement of the embargo must be legalized. The illegal enforcement by the regular army on a routine basis and the illegal control of the collectors' discretionary power to detain were among the matters in the President's mind.

He instructed Gallatin to prepare a bill for Congress, remedying the "defect" experience had revealed. He ticked off a few reminders: "Mandamus. The discretion of the collector expressly subjected to instructions from hence. To seize all suspected deposits. Bonds to be equal to what cargoes would sell for in the highest foreign market, &c. Such other amendments as have occurred to you."[33] After consultations with the President, Gallatin prepared for Congress' consideration a set of complex recommendations that disclosed an ugly Jeffersonian spirit.

Prohibitive penalties, many times the combined value of ship and cargo, were prescribed for violations. Oppressive rules regulated owners, masters, and shippers. One particularly ingenious device recommended by Gallatin to Senator Giles was calculated to prevent a vessel, cleared for an American port, from trading at sea or putting in at a foreign port. If the cargo cleared at the port of debarkation did not match the manifests, "neither capture, distress, nor any other accident should be admitted as a plea, or given in evidence on trial."[34] The beauty of this proposal, from the standpoint of the Administration, was that it insured convictions, for the parties on trial were to be denied the opportunity of offering in their defense the only kind of evidence that might establish their innocence.[35]

Distrust of courts and juries, as well as of everyone engaged in coastal trade, led to an abandonment of established rules of evidence. An equally harsh rule recommended to Congress was that the last registered owner of a vessel be automatically subject to all penalties for any infraction of the laws. Thus the inquiry at a trial was to turn on the mere fact of ownership rather than on complicity in the alleged violation. An innocent owner might be held guilty of acts committed by his captain and crew. In cases where the ship or cargo had been sold and the registry of the customs house did not show the fact of sale till long after, as was the usual practice, a former owner could be held guilty. Complicated administrative regulations for enforcement were of the "odious" nature that Gallatin had warned Jefferson would be necessary.

To Senator Giles, the Secretary of the Treasury admitted that one recommendation would create "an arbitrary power to seize unusual deposits" anywhere.[36] By the Fourth Embargo Act, collectors could seize suspicious stockpiles only at points adjacent to foreign territory. Gallatin now proposed to extend the power of seizure to all districts and, like the detention power, to place it "under the control of the President, [to] be executed only in conformity with such general rules as he would prescribe." The recommendation, in effect, suspended the Fourth Amendment's guarantee against unreasonable searches and seizures and substituted executive discretion for search warrants issued by the courts.

Other noteworthy recommendations called for larger cutters, manned by crews of fifteen to thirty, for use in the enforcement of the embargo; for extension of the detention power to land vehicles; for punishment of "every degree of opposition to the laws which falls short of treason"; for protecting collectors against suits in state courts "by making it penal for any sheriff or other person to execute the same, or in any manner to attempt to take property which . . . is in the collector's possession"; and for easing the means by which the "physical force of the country" could be utilized for enforcement.[37]

The Fifth Embargo Act was fully debated by Congress. Arrogant in the knowledge that they controlled large majorities in both houses, Administration spokesmen submitted to a relentless forensic drubbing. Every provision of each section of the long bill was denounced as tyrannous, and too often the minority spokesmen were accurate. Sections nine and eleven were particularly singled out, in the words of Senator White of Delaware, "as laying the whole country under military law —as nothing less than a declaration of war, on the part of the Government, against our own citizens."[38] The ninth section embodied those arbitrary powers of seizure of which Gallatin had spoken, while the eleventh provided the military force that made them enforceable.

By the eleventh section, the President or anyone to whom he delegated the power might "employ such part of the land or naval forces of the United States, or of the militia thereof, as may be judged necessary for the purpose, in conformity with the provisions of this and other acts respecting the embargo." This was the only time in American history that the President was empowered to use the army for routine or day-by-day execution of the laws. The necessity of proclaiming the existence of an insurrection, or domestic violence, or obstructions by combinations too powerful to suppress by normal civil procedures was abolished. Armed force was to be the new rule, not the exception. Little wonder that Senator Goodrich declared that the bill "strikes at the vital principles of our republican system" by placing the nation "in time of peace under military law."[39] His colleague from Connecticut, Representative Benjamin

Talmadge, hysterically warned against a "military dictator."[40]

Section nine as passed by the Senate made money and any articles of domestic growth or manufacture subject to seizure on the collector's suspicion that they were "intended for exportation." The unrestricted seizure power, applicable to all places, times, and commodities, and backed by military power, provoked the minority to frenzied denunciations that were wholly justified. Collectors, raged Federalist speakers, with or without a detachment of soldiers, without search warrants, without proof, from suspicion only, or perhaps from resentment, prejudice, or party spirit, might invade homes and places of business and ransack studies, wagons, or ships, to seek incriminating evidence and seize any property. The property seized was not illegally possessed; it need merely be suspected of being intended, at some future time, for export. Search, seizure, and arrests would be based on the expectation, unproved and, more often than not, unprovable, that an act in violation of the embargo laws *might* be committed. The privilege against self-incrimination was rendered meaningless; the right to trial by jury made a farce; the protection against property being taken without due process of law ignored; and the freedom from unreasonable searches and seizures abolished.[41]

Against this irrefutable proof of the unconstitutionality of section eleven, the Administration forces in the House weakened a bit and passed an amendment that prevented the search-and-seizure power from being used in homes or anywhere on land, excepting vehicles "apparently on their way" toward foreign territories "or toward a place whence such articles are intended to be exported." The amendment did more to assuage the consciences of the majority than it did to appease the minority, who regarded it as a sponge to dry an unconstitutional ocean. But the bill passed the House by a vote of 71 to 32 and was signed into law by the President on January 9, 1809.[42] To this day it remains the most repressive and unconstitutional legislation ever enacted by Congress in time of peace. No peacetime President ever sought, or received, such a vast concentration of power as did Jefferson and at the expense of provisions in the Bill of Rights which he himself once advocated as necessary checks against tyranny.[43]

In the midst of the House debate on the force act of 1809, a resolution was moved to raise and equip fifty thousand soldiers for a period of two years.[44] The resolution may have been intended to blackjack a panicky opposition into submission out of fear that things could be much worse. The Federalist speakers who opposed the bill pointed out that the President himself had done no more than ask Congress to consider measures needful for defense. He had not even intimated a need for further expansion of the peacetime army, let alone an expansion of the magnitude proposed. Congressman Eppes, in a lengthy reply, defended the resolution against its critics, without actually justifying the mammoth proportions of the proposed army.[45] A bill was engrossed, proceeded to a third reading, and was seriously debated, with support by Administration forces, even *after* the enactment of the Fifth Embargo.[46] In the course of the debates, the fact emerged that the Administration did indeed back the bill in all seriousness. It had originated in a recommendation of the Secretary of War, indicating presidential endorsement.[47] The

House, however, adjourned without taking a vote on the measure.

Had the bill passed, it would have been an incongruous complement to the Fifth Embargo Act which, for all its bristling militarism, was ironically intended to enforce a policy of national passive resistance as a means of averting war. Military preparedness against France and England was actually a policy of realism. In the absence of the embargo policy, multiplying the size of the army by fivefold would have made good sense. But in conjunction with the embargo policy, particularly the Fifth Embargo Act, the army bill was a yardstick of the Jefferson spirit in the winter of 1808–09. If the Fourth Embargo had carried the Administration to the brink of a grinding, ironhanded rule, the Fifth Embargo carried it over the brink.

As a means of peaceably coercing European powers to rescind their harmful decrees against American commerce, the embargo policy was a total failure. It failed as dismally as a domestic measure if judged by its politically divisive and harmful economic consequences, its brutal assaults on personal and property rights, and its tragic corruption of Jeffersonian principles. Within a month of the passage of the last force act, Congressmen under enormous pressure from their constituents began abandoning the Administration. The final turn of the screw had cracked party discipline.

Jefferson showed surprise at his unexpected rout. "I thought," he wrote, "Congress had taken their ground firmly for continuing their embargo . . . But a sudden and unaccountable revolution of opinion took place the last week, chiefly among the New England and New York members, and in a kind of panic they voted the

4th of March [Jefferson's final day in office] for removing the embargo."[48] So little was he aware of the actual state of public opinion. Shortly before leaving office, he confided to an old friend that he looked eagerly forward "to my family, my books and farms . . . Never did a prisoner, released from his chains, feel such relief as I shall on shaking off the shackles of power."[49] The nation was equally relieved.

✧ Chapter Seven ✧

On Guard against Political Heresies: Of Hume and the University of Virginia

BACK among his books, the former President zestfully resumed his studies in a dozen realms of knowledge, becoming once again the philosopher of liberty. But the fires of his faith in his fellow men's judgment burned a bit lower and at times flickered as if dampened by disillusion. Jefferson was still usually buoyant, optimistic, and trusting on any question about the capacity of people to choose wisely when given all the facts. But there were moments when doubt induced him to try to stack the cards to insure his bets. His doubt disclosed itself even in the area of intellectual liberty and academic freedom where his faith might least be expected to waver.

The ultimate victory of truth over falsehood in any fair encounter was one of Jefferson's cardinal beliefs. It was a foundation of his willingness to tolerate error. A man of deep convictions, whether in matters of religion, politics, law, science, history, philosophy, or even architecture, he was a rugged, often passionate, advocate. It was not his nature to feign unconcern when exposed to an opinion that he thought erroneous. He answered back, almost invariably with reasoned judgment, not because he was contentious but because he cared strongly. He was not indifferent to error, only respectful of the rights of others to be mistaken. That is why he tolerated, though only tolerated, error of opinion. Politics frequently strained his toleration to the breaking point. But where scholarship was involved, he was a model of intellectual fairness and rectitude. It was all the more disconcerting, therefore, to find him flirting with the censorship of books.

Jefferson, more strongly than most, was afflicted with that occupational vanity of intellectuals: the notion that reading could profoundly influence men's ideas. He was especially concerned about the reading matter of young men whose superior education destined them for leadership in American life. History, thought Jefferson, colored their political outlook. He wanted citizens who could think for themselves, but he also wanted them to think republican thoughts and to support the cause of liberty as he understood it. One of the intellectual titans who, he believed, stood athwart his objective was the English historian and philosopher David Hume. Another was the oracle of the common law, Sir William Blackstone. Both had the unhappy facility of converting their readers to tory doctrines.[1] Fortunately, Blackstone could be studied after exposure to Coke—"a sounder whig never wrote";[2] moreover, there was an American edition of Blackstone by St. George Tucker, a Republican jurist of Virginia who had thoughtfully written elaborate appendixes that made essential corrections to the more seductive of Blackstone's erroneous principles.[3] To counteract Hume's pernicious influence, however, was a nearly insurmountable problem to which Jefferson addressed himself for many years without success.

In 1807, when answering a young man who had requested the President's opinion about the best books on social and political subjects, Jefferson recommended Locke, Sydney, Priestley, Beccaria, Smith, and Say, but he was stumped when it came to a history of Great Britain which he thought vital to an understanding of American government. "There is," he wrote, "no general history of that country which can be recommended." "The elegant one of Hume seems intended to disguise and discredit the good principles of the government, and is so plausible and pleasing in its style and manner, as to instil its errors and heresies insensibly into the minds of unwary readers." However, a certain Englishman named John Baxter, noted the President, had "performed a good operation" on Hume: "wherever he has found him endeavoring to mislead, by either the suppression of a truth or by giving it a false coloring, he has changed the text to what it should be, so that we may properly call it Hume's history republicanised."[4]

In the quiet of his Monticello study, during the years of retirement, Jefferson worried from time to time about the injurious influence of Hume on the minds of impressionable young readers. In 1810 he first determined to do something about an intolerable situation. The solution, he was convinced, lay in making widely available to American readers the "republicanised" version. He urged his old friend William Duane, an editor and publisher in the business of "printing useful works," to publish Baxter's edition of Hume. Jefferson's letter showed his willingness to be a party to intellectual deception. In the case of Hume, he feared that truth would not best error in a fair encounter and therefore needed a slight advantage.

The cause was surely a great one, for as he explained to Duane, "Our laws, language, religion, politics and manners are so deeply laid in English foundations, that we shall never cease to consider their history as a part of ours, and to study ours in that as its origin." But who was the pre-eminent and most popular English historian? "Every one knows that judicious matter and charms of style have rendered Hume's history the manual of every student." Jefferson himself had "devoured" Hume when young and he remembered well "the length of time, the research and reflection which were necessary to eradicate the poison it had instilled into my mind." Hume was an "apologist" for the Stuarts, "advocated all their enormities," and even depicted the Saxon and Norman periods "with the same perverted view."

The problem was that Hume "still continues to be put into the hands of all our young people, and to infect them with the poison of his own principles of government. It is this book which has undermined the free principles of the English government, has persuaded readers of all classes . . . and has spread universal toryism over the land." Baxter, Jefferson urged, "has hit on the only remedy the evil admits. He had taken Hume's work, corrected in the text his misrepresentations, supplied the truths which he suppressed, and yet has given the mass of the work in Hume's own words . . . I cannot say that his amendments are either in matter or manner in the fine style of Hume. Yet they are often unperceived." Baxter's work was rare in England and could not be found in America. The copy in his possession, Jefferson declared, might be the only one in the country. "Can we not have it re-printed here?"[5]

Duane, no doubt for commercial reasons rather than from scholarly integrity, was not interested in the politically bowdlerized and secretly emended abridgment of Hume. But Jefferson's obsession with the menace to republican purity did not abate. He exhorted correspondents to read Baxter and continued to denounce Hume as the "great apostle of Toryism." His fear was that from English toryism, the inevitable result of reading Hume when young, one drifted easily into the camp of American toryism.[6] This belief, however exaggerated, was innocent. But "the only remedy" that Jefferson thought possible ran counter to the canons of scholarship and of intellectual liberty.

In 1818 he made to Mathew Carey, an important publisher, the same proposal he had made to Duane: publication of Baxter's version of Hume. Jefferson's endorsement of Baxter's methods was appalling. Baxter, he informed Carey, "gives you the text of Hume, purely and verbally, till he comes to some misrepresentation or omission . . . he then alters the text silently, makes it what truth and candor say it should be, and resumes the original text again, as soon as it becomes innocent, without having warned you of your rescue from misguidance." The intellectual deception appealed to Jefferson: "And these corrections are so cautiously introduced that you are rarely sensible of the momentary change of your guide. You go on reading true history as if Hume himself had given it."[7] Neither Carey nor Thomas W. White, the next publisher to whom Jefferson appealed, adopted the Baxter project.[8] In the end, truth in a perverse sort of way conquered the Baxter-Jefferson error.

Jefferson's limited career as a censor was renewed in connection with the University of Virginia. If there was ever a place where Baxter's Hume was a libel on scholarship and a subversion of the principle of freedom of the mind, it was a university. But it was in the University of Virginia, above all other places, where Jefferson believed it was most important to load the dice in favor of the right opinions. The open market place of ideas, which had been a hallowed libertarian principle since the publication of *Areopagitica,* seemed too chancy, when the minds of the next generation's leaders were at stake. A man of experience who knew political truth and was devoted to it as the only salvation for the future of republicanism, Jefferson sought to minimize the exposure of the impressionable to baleful influences. Choosing texts and teachers with a view to their political reliability was a delicate business, but Jefferson was up to it.

As the founder and rector of the university, Jefferson held a commanding position to shape its curriculum, staff, and library. Censorship in the form of prohibited reading was unthinkable. But the judicious choice of required texts and the careful appointment of professors served his purpose and fitted his style. Indirection, finesse, and subtlety were almost always characteristic of the way he worked. Wanting Baxter on the shelves and a part of the history curriculum was not a small thing in Jefferson's mind. Hume, he warned, had "revolutionized the public sentiment" of England "more completely than the standing armies could ever have done." Worse still, from reading Hume "it is an easy step to American Toryism."[9]

But Baxter was insufficient insurance against the possibility that the university's graduates might become contaminated by the party dogmas of Alexander Hamilton and John Marshall. Positive measures were needed to produce true political orthodoxy. Jefferson sought not simply the proscription of Tory or Federalist ideas; he wanted the university to become an instrument of his party and to indoctrinate Republicanism as he understood it. However, the partisanship of the university was to be a function of its law school only, for it was there that "the principles of government and political economy" were to be taught; it was there that future statesmen were to be trained.[10]

Jefferson's zeal in building the law school was that of a political missionary. His educational plans took form in the context of his political thought. In his old age he wrote many eloquent and frequently quoted letters on the virtues of democracy and on his faith in the people. But he also wrote many others that showed him as a crabbed and distrustful old man with little faith in the new nationalism or growing authority of the federal government, despite the fact that the nationalism was the expression of the mass of American people and the federal government a major instrument of their democratic aspirations. Jefferson himself had exercised powers of such scope and force as were undreamed of by John Marshall or John Quincy Adams. Yet he plunged from the presidency to a carping criticism of the federal government in a single degeneration. By the 1820's he had become a Southern apologist who from one side of his mouth spoke of the earth as belonging to the living and from the other espoused dead doctrines that helped breed death a generation later. His judgment had become so smothered by localism and strict construction that he could praise John Taylor's bitter, narrow-minded book on the Constitution as containing "the true political faith," to which every republican should steadfastly hold. *Constructions Construed,* he wrote, "should be put in the hands of all our functionaries, authoritatively, as a standing instruction, and true exposition of our Constitution, as understood at the time we agreed to it."[11]

To his old friend William Giles, Jefferson wrote deploring the "rapid strides with which the federal branch of our government is advancing towards the usurpation of all the rights reserved to the States, and the consolidation in itself of all powers, foreign and domestic." Congress and President Adams were equally guilty with Chief Justice Marshall. The bill of particulars in Jefferson's indictment showed how warped his judgment and constricted his national vision had become. "Under the power to regulate commerce," wrote the author of the embargo, "they assume indefinitely that also over agriculture and manufactures." His real complaint was that commerce was the beneficiary of national policy. "Under the authority to establish post roads," he continued, as if forgetting his bold purchase of the Louisiana Territory, "they claim that of cutting down mountains for the construction of roads, of digging canals . . . and whatsoever they shall think, or pretend will be for the general welfare."

The worst of it was that the Constitution could not be preserved by "reason and argument" because Congress was beyond hope. "The representatives chosen by ourselves? They are joined in the combination, some from incorrect views of government, some from corrupt ones, sufficient voting together to outnumber the sound parts." Should the situation continue, the only choice left would be between "dissolution of our Union . . . or submission to a government without limitation of powers. Between these two evils, when we must make a choice, there can be no hesitation."[12]

The same letter quite significantly alluded to Jefferson's hope for the University of Virginia. In twelve or fifteen years, he expected that "a majority of the rulers of our State will have been educated here. They will carry hence the correct principles of our day."[13] This was a recurrent theme in Jefferson's thought. He had become convinced that northern universities taught Federalist or "consolidationist" principles of politics and constitutionalism. Before his own university got under way, he sent his grandson to South Carolina College "rather than anywhere northwardly."[14] To State Senator Joseph C. Cabell, an old friend closely associated with him in the founding of the University of Virginia, he lamented that a shortage of funds would enable the new school to begin with only six professors, with the result that Harvard would "still prime it over us with her twenty professors. How many of our youths she has now, learning the lessons of anti-Missourianism, I know not . . . These will return home, no doubt, deeply impressed with the sacred principles of our Holy Alliance of restrictionists."[15]

To another old Virginia friend who was also a member of the original Board of Visitors, Jefferson explained the mission of the university in purely sectional terms. "The line of division lately marked out between different portions of our confederacy," he confided, "is such as will never, I fear, be obliterated, and we are now trusting to those who are against us in position and principle, to fashion to their own form the minds and affections of our youth." He estimated that "we" sent five hundred "of our own sons" yearly to Northern schools where they were "imbibing opinions and principles in discord with those of their own country. This canker is eating on the vitals of our existence, and if not arrested at once, will be beyond remedy."[16] The remedy was the University of Virginia, particularly its law school.

To James Madison, still another member of the university's Board of Visitors, Jefferson in the last year of his life sent a letter which frankly voiced his hopes for the school's role as a political seminary. "In the selection of our Law Professor," he wrote, "we must be rigorously attentive to his political principles." By way of explanation, he reminded Madison that when Sir Edward Coke's works were the elementary texts of law students in the days before the Revolution, "our lawyers were then all Whigs," because Coke maintained "orthodox doctrines of the British constitution" or what was then called "English liberties." But when Coke "got out of fashion, and the honeyed Mansfieldism of Blackstone became the students' hornbook, from that moment, that profession (the nursery of our Congress) began to slide into toryism, and nearly all the young brood of lawyers now are of that hue." They might suppose themselves to be Whigs, Jefferson declared, only because they no longer knew what "Whigism or republicanism" meant. "It is in our seminary," he concluded, "that the vestal flame is to be kept alive; from thence it is to spread anew over our own and the sister States. If we are true and vigilant in our trust, within a dozen or twenty years a majority of our own legislature will be from one school, and many disciples will have carried its doctrines home with them to their several States, and will have leavened thus the whole mass."[17]

This was not the magnanimous Jefferson of the First Inaugural Address speaking. That Jefferson had announced that every difference of opinion was not a difference of principle, and that though Americans might call their parties by different names, all were "brethren of the same principle. We are all Republicans, we are all Federalists." The aged Jefferson had soured. He was a strong supporter of the party system on the theory that in its absence "some more dangerous principle of division will take its place."[18] But he feared and despised the opposition.

When Jefferson spoke of Whigs and Tories, he had in mind the parties then existing in the United States. Their names might change, he observed, but not their principles. The opposition in the 1820's was still the old promonarchist party that distrusted the people. Monarchism having been trounced in America, the "same party takes now what they deem the next best ground, the consolidation of the government" by concentrating all power in Washington at the expense of the rights of the states. The party names changed—"Whigs, Liberals, Democrats, call them what you please" versus "Tories, Serviles, Aristocrats, etc."—but the division "now existing in the United States" was the old division of "Whig and Tory, or according to our denominations of republican and federal."[19]

When, therefore, Jefferson spoke of the law school of the University of Virginia as a seedbed of future political leaders of Whig persuasion, he meant the school to be an arm of his own party. He was seeking to proscribe the teaching of ideas antithetical to his own views of the federal system. The school was not to teach both Federalist and Republican views objectively or to avoid altogether a study of the American party system; it was to indoctrinate loyalty to Republicanism.

Every man considered for the law post of the university was regarded as a strict constructionist, states' rights advocate of the old Dominion school: Thomas Cooper, Francis Walker Gilmer, Henry St. George Tucker, Philip P. Barbour, Peter Carr, William Wirt, and John Taylor Lomax. The last-named accepted the job after there had been a diligent search for a man of safe political doctrines who combined legal learning and a broad cultural background. Considerable difficulties were experienced in securing the services of the right man for the post, for one after the other declined. At one point the hideous possibility arose that no one but a Federalist would accept appointment. Alarmed, Jefferson wrote extraordinary letters, in almost identical words, to Joseph C. Cabell and James Madison who were members of the university's Board of Visitors. In most "public seminaries," he explained, textbooks were usually prescribed by authority of the trustees. He did not propose that this practice be followed "in our University," because the trustees or visitors did not know enough about the various branches of learning. The choice of textbooks should therefore be left to the professors as a rule.

> But there is one branch in which we are the best judges, in which heresies may be taught, of so interesting a character to our own State and to the United States, as to make it a duty in us to lay down the principles which are to be

taught. It is that of government. Mr. Gilmer being withdrawn, we know not who his successor may be. He may be a Richmond lawyer, or one of that school of quondam federalism, now consolidation. It is our duty to guard against such principles being disseminated among our youth, and the diffusion of that poison, by a previous prescription of the texts to be followed in their discourses. I therefore enclose you a resolution which I think of proposing at our next meeting, strictly confiding it to your own knowledge alone, and to that of Mr. Loyall, to whom you may communicate it, as I am sure it will harmonize with his principles. I wish it to be kept to ourselves, because I have always found that the less such things are spoken of beforehand, the less obstruction is contrived to be thrown in their way. I have communicated it to Mr. Madison.[20]

Cabell replied that he and George Loyall would support Jefferson's "resolution relative to the text books on government," but Madison interposed several expediential objections. Madison did not fundamentally disagree with Jefferson's objectives. He too believed that the university should be a "nursery of Republican patriots as well as genuine scholars."[21] He described a candidate for the sensitive law school post as a "convert to the constitutionality of canals" but in all other respects an adherent "to the Virginia Creed of which he had been a warm advocate."[22] Madison, however, objected to partisanship that was too blatant and might discredit the university. He was also far more realistic in his understanding that a prescription of texts by no means insured the desired results and was secondary in importance to getting the right faculty.

Unfortunately the resolution proposed by Jefferson has been lost. An attempt to reconstruct it from Madison's reply and the resolution finally adopted by the

Board of Visitors depends too much on conjecture to be reliable. It is evident, however, that Madison thought Jefferson to have gone too far. Characteristically Madison re-expressed Jefferson's thoughts in muted and fairly unobjectionable terms. He agreed, for example, that "the true doctrines of liberty, as exemplified in our Political System, should be inculcated on those who are to sustain and may administer it." But he thought it difficult to find books that would be "both guides & guards for the purpose." Sydney and Locke, whom Jefferson had recommended as required reading, might inspire a love of free government but could afford no aid in guarding against violations of American constitutions. The same observation applied to the Declaration of Independence and certainly *The Federalist,* which was subject to "misconstructions" and was differently understood by the rival parties. Some universities required students to read *The Federalist,* "but probably at the choice of the Professors, without any injunction from the superior authority."

As for Jefferson's final recommendation, "the Virginia Document of 1799," Madison modestly thought there might "be more room for hesitation." He himself was the author of that document which had originally appeared as a brilliant party tract of some eighty pages.[23] He referred to it as being "of local origin & having reference to a state of parties not yet extinct." To make it required reading in a school of law, he remarked, "might induce the more bigoted to withhold from it their sons, even when destined for other than the studies of the Law School." He doubted that all members of the party subscribed to it "on every point," and wondered whether all the members of the Board did.[24]

In "framing a political creed," Madison admitted, a very general statement would not answer the purpose, while one in particular terms would divide and exclude. He thought it best to avoid extremes; a statement of "Standards without requiring an unqualified conformity to them" might give them "authority with the Students" and "controul or counteract deviations of the Professor." He had therefore taken the liberty of redrafting Jefferson's statement "with a view to relax the absoluteness of its injunction," and he had also added to the list of required texts the Inaugural Address and the Farewell Address of George Washington. "They may help down what might be less readily swallowed." The "most effectual safeguard against heretical intrusions into the School of Politics," he concluded, "will be an able & orthodox Professor."[25]

Jefferson, immediately sensing the wisdom of Madison's criticism, accepted his amendments. The Board of Visitors, meeting on a day when Adams was inaugurated President of the United States, passed a resolution announcing its obligation to "pay especial attention to the principles of government which shall be inculcated" in the university. Nothing would be taught contrary to the state or federal constitutions as "genuinely based, in the common opinion." Therefore, Locke's *Essay on Civil Government,* Sydney's *Discourses,* The Declaration of Independence, *The Federalist* (an authority on the "genuine meaning" of the United States Constitution), Madison's *Report* of 1799, and Washington's Farewell Address, would constitute the texts and documents of the school of law "on the subject of civil polity."[26]

The seemingly innocuous preamble to the prescription of specific documents as texts must be read in the context of Jefferson's narrowly pro-Southern views, his aim to make the university an instrument of Republicanism, his desire to arrest the "canker" resulting from exposure of young Southerners to Northern opinions in Northern schools, and his reiterated intention of preventing the diffusion of political "poison" by a Federalist professor.

Jefferson had begun his plans for the University of Virginia with the usual libertarian aspirations that characterized his memorable utterances: "This institution," he wrote, "will be based on the illimitable freedom of the human mind. For here we are not afraid to follow the truth wherever it may lead, nor to tolerate any error so long as reason is left free to combat it."[27] Six years later and only a few months before his death, he viewed the law school as the place from which the path of future generations would be lit by the vestal flame of political partisanship rather than by truth or unfettered inquiry. By way of extenuation, it should be added, the law school was no more partisan than its Northern counterparts, and the University of Virginia, as a whole, was as free as any institution of higher learning that had been established in the nation.

⟡ Chapter Eight ⟡

Jefferson as a Libertarian: Conclusions on the Darker Side

A FEW years after Jefferson's death, John Quincy Adams, upon reading Jefferson's *Autobiography*, yielded to his censorious and cantankerous nature. Jefferson, confided Adams to his diary, told nothing that was not creditable to him, as if he had always been right. Yet he had an "infidel philosophy," "pliability of principle," a "treacherous" memory, a "double dealing character," and was so filled with "deep duplicity" and "insincerity" that in deceiving others, "he seems to have begun by deceiving himself." The curious thing about this massive indictment, which was founded on just enough shreds of truth not to be utterly ridiculous, was that Adams spiced it with a dash of credit and a pinch of praise. Even from his jaundiced view, Jefferson was a great patriot with an "ardent passion for liberty and the rights of man."[1] Thus the image of Jefferson as the apostle of freedom had formed even in his own time.

Unlike the Liberty Bell, that image never tarnished or cracked in any serious way. After all, nations live by symbols and have a need for vital illusions. Thomas Jefferson was by no means ill-suited for the symbolic role in which he has been cast by American history. It was a role that he had cast for himself when he left instructions for the epitaph bearing testimony to the three achievements by which he wished "most to be remembered":

Here was buried
Thomas Jefferson
Author of the Declaration of American Independence
of the Statute of Virginia for religious freedom
& Father of the University of Virginia

The words chosen for inscription on the Jefferson Memorial—"I have sworn upon the altar of God, eternal hostility against every form of tyranny over the mind of man"—reflect his enduring spirit and will speak to mankind as long as liberty is cherished on earth. At the dedication of the shrine built by a grateful nation, President Franklin Roosevelt in 1943 quite naturally discoursed on "Thomas Jefferson, Apostle of Freedom." "We judge him," declared Roosevelt, "by the application of his philosophy to the circumstances of his life. But in such applying we come to understand that his life was given for those deeper values that persist throughout all time."[2] The sentiment was a noble one, poetically true. But it was not the whole historical truth.

When judged by his application of "his philosophy to the circumstances of his life," a fair enough test, the saintly vapors that veil the real Jefferson clear away. He himself hated hagiolatry. Posterity, about which he cared so much, had a greater need for a realistic understanding of their heritage than for historical fictions paraded as "images." Jefferson was not larger than life; he was human and held great power. His mistaken judgments were many, his failings plentiful. Much of

Jefferson that passed for wisdom has passed out of date. He was, to be sure, a libertarian, and American civil liberties were deeply in his debt. But he was scarcely the constantly faithful libertarian and rarely, if ever, the courageous one.

The finest moments of American liberty occurred when men defied popular prejudices and defended right and justice at the risk of destroying their own careers. Thus John Adams, at a peak of passionate opposition to the British, defended the hated redcoats against a charge of murder growing out of the Boston Massacre. By contrast Thomas Jefferson never once risked career or reputation to champion free speech, fair trial, or any other libertarian value. On many occasions he was on the wrong side. On others he trimmed his sails and remained silent.

As Secretary of State Jefferson signed the proclamation against the Whiskey Rebels;[3] as Vice President and presiding officer of the Senate, he signed the warrant of arrest for William Duane for a seditious contempt of that august body.[4] Jefferson chose the easy path of lawful performance of his duties instead of conscientious opposition on the ground that liberty and justice were being victimized. In neither case did he speak out *publicly*. He signed in silence and characteristically complained in his private correspondence about the government's abridgments of freedom. His opposition to the Alien and Sedition Acts is famous: what is not so well known is that he never publicly declared his opposition during the period of hysteria. He kept his participation in the Kentucky Resolutions of 1798–99 a secret. In the winter of liberty's danger there was the greatest need for the heated and undisguised voice of dissent to be heard in the land.

Any depiction of Jefferson as the nearly faultless civil libertarian, the oracle of freedom's encyclicals and model of its virtues, should provoke a critical reader who is reasonably aware of human frailties—from which political figures are not notably exempt—to react like Brete Harte's M'liss. Upon being told that the sun had obeyed Joshua's command to stand still in the heavens, she slammed her astronomy book shut with the defiant assertion, "It's a damned lie. I don't believe it." Jefferson was no demigod. That he was a party to many abridgments of personal and public liberty should neither shock nor surprise. It would have been surprising had he not on occasion during his long career taken his hatchet in hand and cut down a few libertarian cherry trees. He said himself that he had been bent like a long bow by irresistible circumstances, his public life being a war against his natural feelings and desires. The compulsions of politics, the exigencies of office, and the responsibilities of leadership sometimes conspired to anesthetize his sensitivity to libertarian values. Nor did his own drives have an opposite effect. He yearned for the contemplative intellectual life but he could not resist the temptations of power. He had as great a need for the means of carrying out policies in the national interest, as he understood it, as he did for the quiet life of scholarship.

He was capable of ruthlessness in the exercise of power. As President he behaved as if compensating for his notorious weakness as wartime governor of Virginia, when constitutional scruples and an inclination to shrink from the harsher aspects of politics had made him incapable of bold leadership. Thereafter he acted as if he had disciplined himself to serve in office with energy and decisiveness, at whatever cost. A hard resolution to lead and triumph certainly characterized his presidency.

Often the master politician, he was not averse to the most devious and harsh tactics to achieve his ends. Usually gentle and amiable in his personal relationships, he possessed a streak of wilfulness that sometimes expressed itself in flaring temper, violence, and toughness. His grandson portrayed him as a "bold and fearless" horseman who loved to ride booted with whip in hand. "The only impatience of temper he ever exhibited," recalled Thomas Jefferson Randolph, "was with his horse, which he subdued to his will by a fearless application of the whip, on the slightest manifestation of restiveness."[5] He rode the nation in the same way, booted and spurred during the embargo days, notwithstanding the fact that one of his most memorable utterances announced his belief that mankind had not been born with saddles on their backs to be ridden booted and spurred by those in power over them.[6]

It is revealing that Jefferson arrogated to himself the power to decide personally how much bread, and with what degree of whiteness, the American people could eat during the embargo.[7] He regulated the nation down to its table fare, despite an aversion to centralized government and a dedication to the belief that domestic concerns were a matter of personal or local government. The eye of President Jefferson was so prying, his enemies bitterly joked, that a baby couldn't be born without clearance from a government customs house.

Practices once reprehended by Jefferson as shocking

betrayals of natural and constitutional rights suddenly seemed innocent, even necessary and salutary, when the government was in his hands. His accession to power seemed to stimulate a fresh understanding of the existence of public dangers requiring forceful measures that often did not result in a union of principle and practice. When, for example, the party faithful were victims of the Sedition Act, unchecked tyranny was abroad in the land with frightening consequences for the future of liberty. When he was in power the uncontrolled licentiousness and malice of the opposition press took on the hideous features of sedition, deserving of a few exemplary prosecutions to protect the public. Jefferson's presidency, particularly the second term which witnessed the federal sedition prosecutions in Connecticut, the Wilkinson-Burr imbroglio and trials, and the five embargo acts, was an obligato on the arts of political manipulation and severity.

Some of his antilibertarianism can be explained by the ironic fact that he was, in the words of a clear-eyed admirer, a "terrifying idealist, tinged with fanaticism."[8] What other sort of man would impersonally applaud a little bloodletting now and then to fertilize the tree of liberty? Jefferson held his convictions with a fierceness that admitted little room for compromise—if he was in a position of power to deny it—and no room for self-doubt. Unduly sensitive to criticism by others, he wore a hair shirt—often a dangerous attire for a politician—which covered a spirit rarely capable of objective disinterestedness.

Jefferson had the mentality and passion of a true believer, certain that he was absolutely right, a marked contrast to the skepticism of modern libertarians such as Justice Oliver Wendell Holmes or Judge Learned Hand. Holmes believed that the first mark of a civilized man was the capacity to doubt his own first principles, while Hand remarked that the spirit of liberty was the spirit which was not too sure that it was right. Jefferson was a product of the eighteenth century which regarded truths as immutable and self-evident. Yet philosophic truths concerning the nature of man or the first principles of government were not on a footing with practical legislation or executive policies. Jefferson had read Locke and the British empiricists as well as the Deists, scientists, and French *philosophes.* He might reasonably have been somewhat more skeptical of the rightness of his own favorite theories that he translated into national policy; he might have been less cocksure, less ready to subcribe to the proposition that certitude was the test of certainty.

In politics, particularly, where the art of the possible is often the highest value, making compromise a necessity, the capacity to doubt one's own convictions is indispensable.[9] The poorest compromise is almost invariably better than the best dictation which leaves little if any scope of freedom to the losing side and corrupts the spirit of those in power. In his old age Jefferson observed wisely: "A government held together by the bands of reason only, requires much compromise of opinion; that things even salutary should not be crammed down the throats of dissenting brethren, especially when they may be put into a form to be willingly swallowed, and that a good deal of indulgence is necessary to strengthen habits of harmony and fraternity."[10] The observation was not an abstract one. Jefferson was arguing at the time in behalf of a constitutional amendment that would authorize the national government—which by then he was denominating the "foreign" department in contrast to the states that composed the "domestic" department—to build roads and canals.[11] He had an utterly exquisite constitutional conscience when he was not in power.

Jefferson's only constitutional qualms during his presidency concerned what he believed to be his questionable authority to purchase Louisiana. He never doubted for a moment the rightness of his behavior during the Burr and embargo episodes. The intensity of his convictions and his incapacity for self-criticism propelled him onward, more resolute than ever in the face of outside criticism. The certainty that he was right, combined with his terrifying idealism, led him to risk the fate of the nation on the chance that an experiment in commercial sanctions might prove a substitute for war. Opposition only goaded him to redouble his efforts to prove himself right. He behaved as if a prisoner of his ideas, or, to put the thought less charitably, as a doctrinaire "tinged with fanaticism."

The self-skeptic, the practical politician, and the democrat conduct themselves otherwise. Any one of them in a position of power tends to operate with an understanding of the necessity of compromise and the obnoxiousness, not to mention the immorality or political stupidity, of cramming legislation "down the throats of dissenting brethren." Legislation, as William James once observed about democracy generally, is a business in which something is done, followed by a pause to see who hollers; then the hollering is relieved as best it can be until someone else hollers. Jefferson, however, was faintly doctrinaire. Exhilarated by the experience of putting an idea in motion and backing it by force, he could not back down or admit that he had been wrong. What counted most was the attainment of his objective, the validation of his conviction, not its impact on those who, failing to appreciate his idealism or personal stake, hollered long and loud. He reacted not by relieving their hollering but by a stretch of the rack that increased their protests and his own power to override them.

Jefferson tended to stretch his political powers as he stretched his mind in intellectual matters, leaving his conscience behind—and sometimes his good sense. His voluminous correspondence showed no hint that he suffered from uncertainty or was tormented by his conscience when he so readily used the army to enforce the embargo and recklessly disregarded the injunctions of the Fourth Amendment. Lincoln in the greatest of all crises in American history had a supreme moral objective as well as a political one to sustain him; but he was constantly racked by self-doubt. The exercise of power, not always constitutionally justifiable, exacted of him a price that included melancholy and an agonized soul. In moments of despair he could doubt that Providence was with him and even that his position was indeed the morally superior one.

The contrast with Jefferson was towering. Thwarted by the courts in Burr's case, Jefferson doubted not himself but the loyalty of the judges. Evasions of the embargo filled him with astonishment not that his policy could have such a result but that the people could be so rankly fraudulent and corrupt. Rumors of resistance were matched by his impulse to crush it by force. There was no inner struggle in Jefferson; the tragedy of his antilibertarianism lacked poignancy. He was oblivious of the tragedy itself, symbolized by that moment of enormity when he approved of the use of any means, even if odious and arbitrary, to achieve his end.

Vanity, the enemy of self-doubt, also played its role in fashioning his darker side. His *amour-propre* prevented him from checking an illiberal act once begun or from admitting his error after the event. Witness his conduct of the Burr prosecutions and the way in which he was driven to defend Wilkinson. His persistent defense of his role in the case of Josiah Philips bears testimony to the same trait. When caught in a flagrancy as when it was revealed that he had hired the journalistic prostitute Callendar to poison the reputations of political opponents, or when he was accused of permitting the sedition prosecutions in Connecticut, he denied the truth. In deceiving others, as John Quincy Adams said, he deceived himself. In deceiving himself he denied himself insight into his abridgments of liberty, though he was acutely perceptive of abridgments by others.

Perhaps the chief explanation of his darker side was his conviction that the great American experiment in self-government and liberty was in nearly constant danger. He completely identified with that experiment, to the point that an attack on him or on the wisdom of his policies quickly became transmuted in his mind as a threat to the security of the tender democratic plant.

During the Revolution, coercive loyalty oaths and proscription of Tory opinions seemed a cheap price to pay when independence was the goal and the outcome was in doubt. The Alien and Sedition Acts, following the enactment of Hamilton's economic policies, forever convinced Jefferson that his political opponents were unalterably committed to the destruction of public liberty in America. In the flush of victory, at that splendid moment of the First Inaugural, he admitted the Federalists into the camp of loyal Americans, but not for long. If the scurrilousness of the Federalists press did not convince him that his magnanimous judgment had been mistaken, opposition to the purchase of Louisiana, coupled to threats of secession, proved his belief that popular government in America was imperiled. Burr's conspiracy brought the ugly menace to a head, justifying drastic countermeasures.

Open defiance of the embargo once again threw the Union's future into grave doubt. That defiance seemed to sabotage majority rule and the only hope of avoiding a war that might end the democratic experiment. In time of such acute crisis, when insurrection existed on a widespread basis and treason itself again loomed, the methods of Draco were tempting. The behavior of the Essex Junto during the War of 1812 reconfirmed Jefferson's worst fears. In the postwar period, from his hilltop at Monticello, he imagined that a monarchistic, clerical cabal had re-formed under a new party guise, employing doctrines of nationalistic consolidation to destroy public liberty.

Over the years he constantly sensed a conspiracy against republicanism. He had a feeling of being besieged by the enemies of freedom who would use it to subvert it. The face of the enemy changed—now that of a Tory; later that of a monarchist, a political priest, an Essex Juntoman, a Quid, or a Burrite; still later that of a judicial sapper-and-miner, an American-system consolidationist, or a Richmond lawyer. The face of the enemy or his name might change, but not his tory principles nor his subversive goal.

To the experiment of democracy in America, as Jefferson called it, he was committed heart, mind, and soul. Believing that experiment to be in grave jeopardy throughout most of his public life, he was capable of ruthlessness in defeating its enemies. His own goal was free men in a free society, but he did not always use freedom's instruments to attain it. He sometimes confused the goal with self-vindication or the triumph of his party. On other occasions instability and a lack of faith were revealed by his doubts of the opposition's loyalty. They were prone, he believed, to betray the principles of the Revolution as expressed in the Declaration of Independence. On still other occasions his eagerness to make America safe for democracy made him forgetful of Franklin's wise aphorism that they who seek safety at the expense of liberty deserve neither liberty nor safety.

The terrible complexities of any major issue, such as Burr's conspiracy or the embargo, particularly as seen from the White House, also help to explain Jefferson's conduct. The strain and responsibilities of the highest office did not stimulate the taking of bold risks on the side of liberty when it seemed to be pitted against national security. Moreover, problems had a way of presenting themselves in a form that mixed conflicting political considerations and obscured clear-cut decisions on libertarian merits. To a mind that was keenly alerted against the conspiracies of Federalist boogeymen and sensed a union between self, party, and nation, the virtue of an independent judiciary became the vice of judicial interference with majority rule; fair trial and a strict interpretation of treason became obstacles to the preservation of the Union; academic freedom became a guise for the dissemination of pernicious doctrines.

Jefferson's darker side derived in part, too, from the fact he had no systematic and consistent philosophy of freedom. He was neither a seminal nor a profound thinker. Part of his genius consisted of his ability to give imperishable expression to old principles and to the deepest yearnings of his fellow citizens. Style, as much as substance, accounted for his staying power. He once defended himself against the accusation that there was not a single fresh idea in the Declaration of Independence by replying that the objective was not to find new principles or arguments never before thought of. It was, rather,

> to place before mankind the common sense of the subject, in terms so plain and firm as to command their assent . . . Neither aiming at originality of principle or sentiment, nor yet copied from any particular and previous writing, it was intended to be an expression of the American mind, and to give to that expression the proper tone and spirit called for by the occasion. All its authority rests then on the harmonizing sentiments of the day.[12]

As a distinguished admirer has written, "Jefferson's seminal achievement was to institutionalize familiar eighteenth-century ideas. He made abstract notions about freedom a dominating faith and thereby the dynamic element in the strivings of men."[13] Moreover he had the superlative talent of organizing a party that might realize his ideals by infusing the new nation with a sense of its special democratic destiny. But his failure to develop a theory of liberty existed and more than likely influenced his antilibertarian thought and action.

In the thousands of pages of his published works there is a notable scarcity of extended treatments on a single subject. Insatiably curious, he knew a little about nearly everything under the sun and a great deal more about law and politics than any man of his time. But in all his writings, over a period of fifty years of high productivity, there is not a single sustained analysis of liberty. He was pithy, felicitous, repetitive, and ever absorbed by the subject, but never wrote a book or even a tract on the meaning of liberty, its dimensions, limitations, and history.

That he made no contribution of this kind is not per se a criticism, for the brief preambles to the Declaration of Independence and the Virginia Statute of Religious Freedom are worth all the books that have been written on liberty. He had not, however, thought through the tough and perplexing problems posed by liberty: the conditions for its survival and promotion; the types of liberty and conflicts between them; the validity of various legal tests for measuring the scope of liberty or its permissible area of operation; and the competing claims of other values.

Jefferson contented himself with a dedication to the general principle, apparently without realizing that general principles do not satisfactorily decide hard, concrete cases. Only in the area of religious liberty did he have a well-developed philosophy, replete with a usable and rationalized test for application to specific cases. There his contribution was pre-eminent, even if derived from English sources. It is significant, however, that he did not apply the overt-acts test outside of the realm of the free exercise of religion. It is even more significant that his literary remains show no evidence that he ever tried to work out a usable test for cases of verbal political crimes.

A philosopher of freedom without a philosophy of freedom, Jefferson was ill-equipped, by his ritualistic affirmations of nebulous and transcendental truths, to confront the problem posed by General Wilkinson's conduct in New Orleans, or the circulation of Hume's history of England in the colleges, or the savage distortions of the opposition press. He reacted expedientially on an *ad hoc* basis and too often hastily. Then his *amour-propre* prevented his candid acknowledgment of a mistaken judgment that demeaned the libertarian values he symbolized to the nation.

Regret and remorse are conspicuously absent from Jefferson's writings, as is reflective reconsideration of a problem. Something in his make-up, more than likely a stupendous ego, inhibited second thoughts. Whether he would deny the plain facts or stubbornly reiterate his original position, he failed to work out fresh guide lines for future conduct. Restatement, not re-evaluation, marked his thinking, and beneath an eloquently turned phrase there lurked a weary, problem-begging cliché. That it was commonplace rarely deprived it of its profundity as a libertarian principle. The "self-evident truths" of the Declaration of Independence will continue to survive all scorn of being "glittering generalities." They tend, however, to overarch real cases.

Jefferson, for example, might declare in his Second Inaugural Address, "If there be any among us who would wish to dissolve this Union or to change its republican form, let them stand undisturbed as monuments of the safety with which error of opinion may be tolerated where reason is left free to combat it." The principle was so broad that it failed to have pertinence for him when he learned that a few "political Priests" and "Federal printers," who had been confident that no federal court would take cognizance of their seditious calumnies, were being criminally prosecuted for their libels against him and his Administration. His awareness of the general distinction between preparation and attempt, or between conspiracy to commit treason and overt acts of treason, escaped application in the case of the Burrites, though not in the case of the Whiskey Rebels. A commitment to the large principle of intellectual liberty had no carry-over when the possibility arose that a "Richmond lawyer" might be appointed professor of law at the University of Virginia.

Maxims of liberty—"glittering generalities"—were frail props for a sound, realistic libertarianism. A mind filled with maxims will falter when put to the test of experience. A mind filled with maxims contents itself with the resonant quality of a noble utterance. Such a mind, although libertarian, cannot produce a libertarian analysis like Madison's *Report* of 1799–1800 on the Alien and Sedition Acts, or Wortman's *Treatise Concerning Political Enquiry.* Jefferson's only tracts and books were *A Summary View of the Rights of British America,* which was a protest against British encroachments on colonial freedom at the eve of the Revolution; *Notes on the State of Virginia,* a guidebook and utilitarian history; the *Manual of Parliamentary Practice;* his *Autobiography* and *The Anas,* which comprise his memoirs; *The Life and Morals of Jesus of Nazareth;* and the philological work, *Essay on Anglo-Saxon.* Despite his interest in freedom, its meaning did not interest him as a subject for even an essay.

A plausible but not wholly convincing explanation of Jefferson's darker side may be founded on the argument that he lived at a time when the understanding of civil liberties was quite different from that of our own. Libertarian standards were also quite new and inchoate, making modern yardsticks of judgment anachronistic as well as unfair and ununderstanding. The first bills of rights did not come into existence until 1776; the national Bill of Rights, not until 1791. The meanings of their provisions were not always clear; their restraints in that formative era constituted an experiment in government. Deviations, inconsistencies, and even gross abridgments were not to be unexpected when experience provided few guides. It was a time of testing, of groping and growth, of trial and error, out of which issued the improvised wisdom of subsequent generations. In any case, counsels of perfection and hindsight come rather cheap when aimed by those not on the firing line or of a later time.

This explanation is certainly a plausible one. Yet it is like the theory that was spoiled by the facts. During the Revolutionary War, only Tory voices—and they were not necessarily wrong—could be found in opposition to loyalty tests, bills of attainder, and suppression of "traitorous" speech. Thereafter there were always respectable, instructive voices, even if heard only in dissent, to sound the alarm against abridgments of liberty. Jefferson needed only to hear or read in order to know that a particular measure could be seriously construed as a threat to the Bill of Rights or the undermining of a libertarian value. For every example of his darker side that has been documented in this book, a congressional speech, a popular tract, a letter, a newspaper editorial, a judicial opinion, or, more likely than not, a pronouncement by Jefferson himself can be adduced to show a judgment of his own time placing his action in an antilibertarian light. By 1800 or thereabouts the standards of his own time did not noticeably differ from those of ours on the kind of civil-liberty questions that he confronted.

Though contributing little to any breakthroughs in libertarian thought, except in the important realm of freedom of religion, Jefferson more than any was responsible for the public sensitivity to libertarian considerations. If the quality of the new nation was measured by the ideals and aspirations that animated it, Jefferson had erred only slightly in confusing his own reputation with that of the democratic experiment. Notwithstanding the reciprocal scurrilities and suspicions of the opposed parties, or more importantly their conflicting interests, Americans were indeed all Federalists, all Republicans. They were equally attached to the "experiment in freedom" and the "empire of liberty." Anyone who depreciates the national commitment to libertarian values, which were bottomed on an extraordinary legal and political sophistication, deprives himself of an understanding of the times—and of the impact of Thomas Jefferson upon it. Jefferson cannot lightly be excused because he lived in an earlier time.

That Jefferson's libertarianism was considerably less than perfect or that his practice flagged behind his faith does not one whit diminish the achievements by which he is best remembered and should be. That he did not always adhere to his libertarian principles does not erode their enduring rightness. It proves only that Jefferson often set the highest standard of freedom for himself and posterity to be measured against. His legacy was the idea that as an indispensable condition for the development of free men in a free society, the state must be bitted and bridled by a Bill of Rights which should be construed in the most generous terms, its protections not to be the playthings of momentary majorities or of those in power.

Bibliography

Notes

Index

Bibliography

PRIMARY SOURCES

Adams, John. *Works; with a Life of the Author,* ed. by Charles Francis Adams (Boston, 1850–1856, 10 vols.), vols. IX–X.

Adams, John Quincy. *Memoirs of John Quincy Adams, Comprising Portions of His Diary from 1795 to 1848,* ed. by Charles Francis Adams (Philadelphia, 1874–1877, 12 vols.), vol. VIII.

[*Annals of Congress*]. *The Debates and Proceedings in the Congress of the United States* (Washington, 1834—).

Anonymous. *The Embargo Laws* (Printed by Cushing and Belcher, Boston, 1809).

——— "Hampden." *A Letter to the President of the United States, Touching the Prosecutions under His Patronage, before the Circuit Court in the District of Connecticut* (New Haven, 1808).

Blake, Francis. *An Examination of the Constitutionality of the Embargo Laws . . . to Which Is Added the Opinion Pronounced by the Court* (Worcester, 1808).

Bentham, Jeremy. *A Fragment on Government* (London, 1776).

[Cabell, Nathan F., ed.]. *Early History of the University of Virginia, As Contained in the Letters of Thomas Jefferson and Joseph C. Cabell* (Richmond, 1856).

Cappon, Lester J., ed. *The Adams-Jefferson Letters: The Complete Correspondence Between Thomas Jefferson and Abigail and John Adams* (Chapel Hill, N.C., 1959, 2 vols).

Chafee, Zechariah, Jr., ed. *Documents on Fundamental Human Rights* (preliminary ed., published in three pamphlets, Cambridge, Mass., 1952), Third Pamphlet.

Dawes, M[anasseh]. *The Deformity of the Doctrine of Libels, and Informations Ex Officio* (London, 1785).

Elliot, Jonathan, ed. *The Debates in the Several State Conventions . . . and Other Illustrations of the Constitution* (Philadelphia, 1941, 2nd ed., rev., 5 vols).

Furneaux, Philip. *An Interesting Appendix to Sir William Blackstone's Commentaries on the Laws of England* (Philadelphia, 1773).

——— *Letters to the Honourable Mr. Justice Blackstone, Concerning His Exposition of the Act of Toleration . . . in His Celebrated Commentaries on the Laws of England* (London, 1771, 2nd ed.).

——— *The Palladium of Conscience* (Philadelphia, 1773).

Gallatin, Albert. *The Writings of Albert Gallatin,* ed. by Henry Adams (Philadelphia, 1879, 3 vols.), vol. I.

[Hay, George]. Hortensius. *An Essay on the Liberty of the Press, Respectfully Inscribed to the Republican Printers throughout the United States* (Philadelphia, 1799, 51 pp. Reprinted in Richmond, 1803, in 30 pp).

——— *An Essay on the Liberty of the Press, Shewing, That the Requisition of Security for Good Behaviour from Libellers, Is Perfectly Compatible with the Constitution and Laws of Virginia* (Richmond, 1803, 48 pp).

Hening, William Waller, ed. *The Statutes at Large, Being a Collection of All the Laws of Virginia, 1619–1792* (Richmond, 1809–1823, 13 vols).

Howell, Thomas Bayly, comp. *A Complete Collection of State Trials to 1783*. Continued by T. J. Howell to 1820 (London, 1816–1828, 34 vols.), vol. XVII.

Jefferson, Thomas. *Notes on the State of Virginia,* ed. by William Peden (Chapel Hill, N.C., 1955).

——— *The Papers of Thomas Jefferson,* ed. by Julian P. Boyd, *et al.* (Princeton, 1950—, 16 vols).

——— *Thomas Jefferson Correspondence Printed from the Originals in the Collection of William K. Bixby,* ed. by Worthington C. Ford (Boston, 1916).

——— *The Writings of Thomas Jefferson,* ed. by Paul Leicester Ford (New York, 1892–1899, 10 vols).

——— *The Writings of Thomas Jefferson,* ed. by Andrew A. Lipscomb and Albert Ellery Bergh (Washington, 1904–1905, 20 vols).

Journals of the Continental Congress, 1774–1789, ed. by Worthington C. Ford (Washington, 1904–1937, 24 vols).

Kippis, Alexander. *A Vindication of the Protestant Dissenting Ministers* (London, 1773).

Madison, James. *Letters and Other Writings of James Madison* (Philadelphia, 1865, 4 vols).

——— *The Papers of James Madison,* ed. by William T. Hutchinson and William M. E. Rachal (Chicago, 1962—, 2 vols).

——— *The Virginia Report of 1799–1800, Touching the Alien and Sedition Laws; Together with the Virginia Resolutions of December 21, 1798, the Debates and Proceedings Thereon, in the House of Delegates in Virginia* (Richmond, 1850).

——— *The Writings of James Madison,* ed. by Gaillard Hunt (New York, 1900–1910, 9 vols).

[Maseres, Francis]. *An Enquiry into the Extent of the Power of Juries, on Trials of Indictments or Informations, for Publishing Seditious, or Other Criminal Writings, or Libels, Extracted from a Miscellaneous Collection of Papers That Were Published in 1776, Intitled, Additional Papers Concerning the Province of Quebec* (Dublin, 1792).

Palmer, William P., *et al.,* eds. *Calendar of Virginia State Papers and Other Manuscripts* (Richmond, 1875–1893, 11 vols.), vols. I–II.

Plumer, William. *William Plumer's Memorandum of Proceedings in the United States Senate,* ed. by Everett Somerville Brown (New York, 1923).

Ratcliffe, Ebenezer. *Two Letters Addressed to the Right Rev. Prelates* (London, 1773).

Robertson, David, ed. *Reports of the Trials of Colonel Aaron Burr, (Late Vice President of the United States,) for Treason, and for a Misdemeanor . . . in the Circuit Court of the United States* (Philadelphia, 1808, 2 vols).

Rutherfurd, Livingston. *John Peter Zenger, His Press, His Trial and a Bibliography of Zenger Imprints. Also a Reprint of the First Edition of the Trial* (New York, 1904).

Smith, William. *Historical Memoirs from 16 March 1763 to 9 July 1776 of William Smith,* ed. by William H. W. Sabine (New York, 1956).

Sowerby, E. Millicent, ed. and comp. *Catalog of the Library of Thomas Jefferson* (Washington, 1952–1959, 5 vols).

Thomson, John. *An Enquiry, Concerning the Liberty, and Licentiousness of the Press, and the Uncontroulable Nature of the Human Mind* (New York, 1801).

Thorpe, Francis Newton ed. *The Federal and State Constitutions, Colonial Charters, and Other Organic Laws* (Washington, 1909, 7 vols).

"Trial of Aaron Burr," *Annals of Congress,* 10th Congress, 1st session, Appendix to Senate Debates, pp. 385–778.

Tucker, St. George, ed. *Blackstone's Commentaries: with notes of reference, to the Constitution and Laws, of the Federal Government of the United States . . . and of the Commonwealth of Virginia. With an appendix to each volume, containing short tracts upon such subjects as appeared necessary to form a connected view of the Laws of Virginia, as a Member of the Federal Union* (Philadelphia, 1803, 5 vols).

Wharton, Francis, ed. *State Trials of the United States during the Administrations of Washington and Adams* (Philadelphia, 1849).

Wortman, Tunis. *Treatise Concerning Political Enquiry, and the Liberty of the Press* (New York, 1800).

SECONDARY SOURCES

Adams, Henry. *History of the United States during the Administrations of Thomas Jefferson and James Madison* (New York, 1889–1891, 9 vols).

Bailyn, Bernard. "Boyd's Jefferson: Notes for a Sketch," *New England Quarterly,* 38:380–400 (Sept. 1960).

Becker, Carl. *The Declaration of Independence* (New York, 1922).

Bestor, Arthur, *et al. Three Presidents and Their Books* (Urbana, Ill., 1955).

Beveridge, Albert J. *The Life of John Marshall* (Boston, 1919, 4 vols.), vol. III.

Bowers, Claude. "Jefferson and Civil Liberty," *Atlantic Monthly,* 191:52–58 (Jan. 1953).

——— *Jefferson in Power: The Death Struggle of the Federalists* (Boston, 1936).

Boyd, Julian P. "The Fear of Ideas," *American Scholar,* 21:413–422 (Autumn 1952).

——— "The Relevance of Thomas Jefferson for the Twentieth Century," *American Scholar,* 22:61–76 (Winter 1952–53).

——— "Subversive of What?" *Atlantic Monthly,* 182:19–23 (Aug. 1948).

——— "Thomas Jefferson and the Police State," *North Carolina Historical Review,* 15:233–253 (April 1948).

——— "Thomas Jefferson's 'Empire of Liberty,'" *Virginia Quarterly Review,* 24:538–554 (Autumn 1948).

Brant, Irving. *James Madison: The Nationalist,* 1780–1787 (Indianapolis, Ind., 1948).

Butts, R. Freeman. *The American Tradition in Religion and Education* (Boston, 1950).

Chafee, Zechariah, Jr. *Three Human Rights in the Constitution* (Lawrence, Kan., 1956).

Chapin, Bradley. "Colonial and Revolutionary Origins of The American Law of Treason," *William and Mary Quarterly,* 17:3–21 (Jan. 1960).

Chinard, Gilbert. *Thomas Jefferson: The Apostle of Americanism* (Ann Arbor, Mich., 1957, 2nd ed., rev.).

Cobb, Sanford H. *The Rise of Religious Liberty in America* New York, 1902).

Commager, Henry Steele. "Jefferson and the Book-Burners," *American Heritage,* 9:65–68 (Aug. 1958).

——— *Majority Rule and Minority Rights* (New York, 1943).

Corwin, Edward S. *The President: Office and Powers, 1787–1948* (New York, 1948).

——— "The Supreme Court as National School Board," *Law and Contemporary Problems,* 14:3–22 (Winter 1949).

Crosskey, William W. *Politics and the Constitution* (Chicago, 1953, 2 vols).

Cummings, Homer and Carl McFarland. *Federal Justice: Chapters in the History of Justice and the Federal Executive* (New York, 1937).

Davis, George B. *A Treatise on the Military Laws of the United States* (New York, 1913, 3rd ed).

Davis, Matthew H. *Memoirs of Aaron Burr* (New York, 1837, 2 vols).

Dumbauld, Edward. *The Declaration of Independence and What It Means Today* (Norman, Okla., 1950).

Eckenrode, H[amilton] J. *The Revolution in Virginia* (Boston, 1916).

——— *The Separation of Church and State in Virginia* (Richmond, 1910).

Frankfurter, Felix. *Of Law and Men: Papers and Addresses of Felix Frankfurter,* ed. by Philip Elman (New York, 1956).

Goebel, Julius, and T. Raymond Naughton. *Law Enforcement in Colonial New York: A Study in Criminal Procedure, 1664–1776* (New York, 1944).

Greene, M. Louise. *The Development of Religious Liberty in Connecticut* (Boston, 1905).

Griswold, A. Whitney. "Thomas Jefferson: Anti-Totalitarian," in Edward N. Saveth, ed., *Understanding the American Past* (Boston, 1954), pp. 178–189.

Harrell, Isaac Samuel. *Loyalism in Virginia: Chapters in the Economic History of the Revolution* (Durham, N.C., 1926).

Hazeltine, John H. *The Declaration of Independence* (New York, 1906).

Honeywell, Roy J. *The Educational Work of Thomas Jefferson* (Cambridge, Mass., 1931).

Hurst, Willard. "Treason in the United States," *Harvard Law Review*, 58:226–272 (Dec. 1944); 395–444 (Feb. 1945); and 806–857 (July 1945).

Hyman, Harold M. *To Try Men's Souls: Loyalty Tests in American History* (Berkeley, Calif., 1959).

James, Charles F. *Documentary History of the Struggle for Religious Liberty in Virginia* (Lynchburg, Va., 1900).

Jennings, Walter Wilson. *The American Embargo, 1807–1809* (Iowa City, Iowa, 1921).

Kimball, Marie. *Jefferson: War and Peace, 1776 to 1784* (New York, 1947).

Koch, Adrienne. *Jefferson and Madison: The Great Collaboration* (New York, 1950).

Koch, Adrienne, and Harry Ammon. "The Virginia and Kentucky Resolutions: An Episode in Jefferson's and Madison's Defense of Civil Liberties," *William and Mary Quarterly*, 3rd ser., 5 (1948): 145–176.

Levy, Leonard W. *Legacy of Suppression: Freedom of Speech and Press in Early American History* (Cambridge, Mass., 1960).

——— "Liberty and the First Amendment, 1790–1800," *American Historical Review*, 68:22–37 (Oct. 1962).

Lingley, Charles Ramsdell. *The Transition in Virginia from Colony to Commonwealth* (New York, 1910).

McCaleb, Walter Flavius. *The Aaron Burr Conspiracy* (New York, 1936).

Malone, Dumas. *Jefferson and His Time:* vol. I, *Jefferson The Virginian* (Boston, 1948), and vol. II, *Jefferson and the Rights of Man* (Boston, 1951).

Mays, David John. *Edmund Pendleton, 1721–1803* (Cambridge, Mass., 1952, 2 vols).

Meade, Robert Douthat. *Patrick Henry: Patriot in the Making* (Philadelphia, 1957).

Meyer, Jacob C. *Church and State in Massachusetts from 1740 to 1833* (Cleveland, 1930).

Morgan, Donald G. *Justice William Johnson, The First Dissenter* (Columbia, S.C., 1954).

Mott, Frank L. *Jefferson and the Press* (Baton Rouge, La., 1943).

Moulton, Sherman R. "A Vermont Treason Trial," Vermont Bar Association, *Proceedings*, 24 (1935):121–141.

Nock, Albert Jay. *Jefferson* (New York, 1926).

O'Neill, James M. *Religion and Education under the Constitution* (New York, 1949).

Parton, James. *Life of Andrew Jackson* (New York, 1861, 3 vols.), vol. I.

Perkins, Bradford. *The First Rapprochement: England and the United States, 1795–1805* (Philadelphia, 1955).

Perry, Ralph Barton. *Puritanism and Democracy* (New York, 1944).

Peterson, Merrill D. *The Jefferson Image in the American Mind* (New York, 1960).

Purcell, Richard J. *Connecticut in Transition, 1775–1818* (Washington, 1918).

Rich, Bennett Milton. *The Presidents and Civil Disorder* (Washington, 1941).

Rosenberger, Francis Coleman. *Jefferson Reader: A Treasury of Writings about Thomas Jefferson* (New York, 1953).

Rowland, Kate Mason. *The Life of George Mason* (New York, 1892, 2 vols).

Schachner, Nathan. *Aaron Burr, A Biography* (New York, 1937).

——— *Thomas Jefferson, A Biography* (New York, 1951, 2 vols).

Scott, Arthur P. *Criminal Law in Colonial Virginia* (Chicago, 1930).

Sears, Louis Martin. *Jefferson and the Embargo* (Durham, N.C., 1927).

Smith, James Morton. *Freedom's Fetters: The Alien and Sedition Laws and American Civil Liberties* (Ithaca, N.Y., 1956).

Stokes, Anson Phelps. *Church and State in the United States* (New York, 1950, 3 vols).

Strickland, Reba C. *Religion and the State in Georgia in the Eighteenth Century* (New York, 1939).

Taylor, Telford. *Grand Inquest: The Story of Congressional Investigations* (New York, 1955).

Trent, W. P. "The Case of Josiah Philips," *American Historical Review*, 1:444–454 (April 1896).

Turner, Jesse. "A Phantom Precedent," *American Law Review*, 48:321–344. (May 1914).

Vagts, Detlev. "Free Speech in the Armed Forces," *Columbia Law Review*, 57 (1957):187–218.

Van Tyne, Claude H. *The Loyalists in the American Revolution* (New York, 1902).

Wandell, Samuel H., and Meade Minnigerode. *Aaron Burr* (New York, 1925, 2 vols).

Warfield, Ethelbert D. *The Kentucky Resolutions of 1798* (New York, 1897).
Warren, Charles. *The Supreme Court in United States History* (Boston, 1923, 3 vols).
Waterman, Julian S. "Thomas Jefferson and Blackstone's Commentaries," *Illinois Law Review,* 27:629–659 (Feb. 1933).
Werline, Albert Warwick. *Problems of Church and State in Maryland during the Seventeenth and Eighteenth Centuries* (South Lancaster, Mass., 1948).
White, Leonard D. *The Jeffersonians. A Study in Administrative History, 1801–1829* (New York, 1956).
Wiener, Frederick Bernays. "Courts-Martial and the Bill of Rights: The Original Practice," *Harvard Law Review,* 72:1–49 (Nov. 1958) and 266–304 (Dec. 1958).
Winthrop, William Woolsey. *Military Law and Precedents* (Boston, 1896, 2nd ed., rev., 2 vols).
Wirt, William. *Sketches of the Life and Character of Patrick Henry* (New York, 1832, 2 vols).

Notes

ONE. THE JEFFERSON IMAGE

1. "Message to Congress in Special Session," July 4, 1861, in Roy P. Basler *et al.*, eds., *The Collected Works of Abraham Lincoln* (New Brunswick, N.J., 1953, 9 vols.), IV, 426.

2. Madison to William Bradford, Jan. 24, 1774, in William T. Hutchinson and William M. E. Rachal, eds., *The Papers of James Madison* (Chicago, 1962—), I, 106 and 107, n. 8.

3. H. J. Eckenrode, *Separation of Church and State in Virginia* (Richmond, Va., 1910), ch. 1, "The Establishment," is the best review of the subject.

4. Hutchinson and Rachal, eds., *Papers of Madison*, I, 170–179, *passim.*

5. Eckenrode, *Separation of Church and State*, pp. 49–53. Charles F. James, ed., *Documentary History of the Struggle for Religious Liberty in Virginia* (Lynchburg, Va., 1900), contains a valuable collection of the source materials. The best collection showing Jefferson's thought and activity on religious liberty during the October 1776 session of the legislature is the group of nine documents under the heading, "Notes and Proceedings on Discontinuing the Establishment of the Church of England," in Julian P. Boyd *et al.*, eds., *The Papers of Thomas Jefferson* (Princeton, N.J., 1950—), I, 525–558. Hereafter cited as Boyd.

6. Eckenrode, *Separation of Church and State*, pp. 58–61.

7. There is no single volume on establishments of religion in early American history. The best comprehensive coverages are in Sanford H. Cobb, *The Rise of Religious Liberty in America* (New York, 1902), and Anson Phelps Stokes, *Church and State in the United States* (New York, 1950, 3 vols.), vol. I, ch. 5. For the history of particular establishments, see: Jacob C. Meyer, *Church and State in Massachusetts from 1740 to 1833* (Cleveland, 1930); M. Louise Greene, *The Development of Religious Liberty in Con-*

necticut (Boston, 1905); Richard J. Purcell, *Connecticut in Transition, 1775–1818* (Washington, 1918); Reba C. Strickland, *Religion and the State in Georgia in the Eighteenth Century* (New York, 1939); and Albert Warwick Werline, *Problems of Church and State in Maryland during the Seventeenth and Eighteenth Centuries* (South Lancaster, Mass., 1948).

8. "A Bill for Establishing Religious Freedom," in Boyd, II, 545–553. Jefferson supported disestablishment as early as June 1776 when he drafted three versions of a state constitution, each including a clause guaranteeing that no person shall be compelled "to frequent or maintain" any religious service or institution. See *ibid.*, I, 344, 353, 363. In addition to the materials cited in Boyd, in note 5, above, an excellent revelation of Jefferson's thinking on religious liberty is in his *Notes on the State of Virginia* (written 1780–1782, published in London, 1787), ed. by William Peden (Chapel Hill, N.C., 1955), Query XVII on Religion, pp. 157–161.

9. Irving Brant, *James Madison: The Nationalist, 1780–1787* (Indianapolis, Ind., 1948), pp. 343–358; and Eckenrode, *Separation of Church and State*, pp. 113–115.

10. Jefferson to the Rev. Samuel Miller, Jan. 23, 1808, in Andrew A. Lipscomb and Albert Ellery Bergh, eds., *The Writings of Thomas Jefferson* (Washington, 1904–1905, 20 vols.), XI, 428–430. Hereafter cited as Lipscomb.

11. Jefferson to Messrs. Nehemiah Dodge, Ephraim Robbins, and Stephen S. Nelson, a Committee of the Danbury Baptist Association, in the State of Connecticut, Jan. 1, 1802, in Lipscomb, XVI, 281–282.

12. James M. O'Neill, *Religion and Education under the Constitution* (New York, 1949), pp. 81–82, 83.

13. Edward S. Corwin, "The Supreme Court as National School Board," *Law and Contemporary Problems*, 14:14 (Winter 1949).

14. Jefferson to Levi Lincoln, Jan. 1, 1802, in Lipscomb, X, 305.

15. See, for example, O'Neill, pp. 76–77, 205–206.

16. Boyd, II, 526–535.

17. *Notes on Virginia*, ed. by Peden, p. 147.

18. Lipscomb, XVII, 425.

19. Boyd, II, 535–542.

20. Jefferson to Joseph C. Cabell, Feb. 22, 1821, in Nathaniel F. Cabell, ed., *Early History of the University of Virginia* (Richmond, 1856), p. 207.

21. *Notes on Virginia*, ed. by Peden, p. 151.

22. Jefferson to Peter Carr, Sept. 7, 1814, in Lipscomb, XIX,

211–221. See also Roy J. Honeywell, *The Educational Work of Thomas Jefferson* (Cambridge, Mass., 1931), pp. 15–16, 39–42; the letter to Carr is reprinted in Appendix E.

23. "Report of the Commissioners appointed to fix the site of the University of Virginia," in Honeywell, *Educational Work of Jefferson,* Appendix J, pp. 256, 249.

24. Jefferson to Thomas Cooper, Nov. 2, 1822, in Lipscomb, XV, 405.

25. Minutes of the Board of Visitors of the University of Virginia, Oct. 7, 1822, in *ibid.,* XIX, 414–416.

26. Jefferson to Cooper, Nov. 2, 1822, in *ibid.,* XV, 405.

27. Minutes of the Board of Visitors of the University of Virginia, Oct. 4, 1824, in *ibid.,* XIX, 449.

28. Jefferson to A. S. Brockenbrough, April 21, 1825, quoted in R. Freeman Butts, *The American Tradition in Religion and Education* (Boston, 1950), p. 129, citing Jefferson Papers, Library of Congress, vol. 229, fol. 40962.

29. *Ibid.,* 130.

30. Merrill D. Peterson, *The Jefferson Image in the American Mind* (New York, 1960), p. 456.

31. Hildreth, *The History of the United States of America* (New York, 1860), VI, 141, quoted in Peterson, *The Jefferson Image,* p. 139.

32. Dumas Malone, *Jefferson The Virginian* (Boston, 1948), p. xiv.

33. Julian P. Boyd, jacket copy for Peterson, *The Jefferson Image.* See also Boyd, I, xi; and articles by Boyd: "Thomas Jefferson and the Police State," *North Carolina Historical Review,* 15:233–253 (April 1948); "Subversive of What?" *Atlantic Monthly,* 182:19–23 (Aug. 1948); "The Fear of Ideas," *American Scholar,* 21:413–421 (Autumn 1952); "The Relevance of Thomas Jefferson for the Twentieth Century," *American Scholar,* 22:61–76 (Winter 1952–53).

34. Peterson, *The Jefferson Image,* p. 456.

35. Jefferson to Dr. James Brown, Oct. 27, 1808, in Lipscomb, XII, 183.

36. Jefferson to Joseph H. Priestly, June 19, 1802, in Lipscomb, X, 324.

37. Jefferson to the Citizens of Washington, March 4, 1809, in Lipscomb, XVI, 347–348.

38. Jefferson to Richard Rush, Oct. 20, 1820, in Lipscomb, XV, 284.

Notes to Chapter Two

TWO. IN TIMES THAT TRIED MEN'S SOULS: THE AMERICAN REVOLUTION

1. *Journals of the Continental Congress,* ed. by Worthington Chauncey Ford *et al.* (Washington, 1904–1937, 24 vols.), IV, 18, Jan. 2, 1776.

2. *Ibid.*, V, 670–671.

3. *Ibid.*, V, 789, section II, article 1, adapted from the same section of the British code of 1774. See *ibid.*, V, 670–671. See also George B. Davis, *A Treatise on the Military Laws of the United States* (New York, 1913, 3rd ed.), 375–376; William W. Winthrop, *Military Law and Precedents* (Boston, 1896, 2nd ed.), *1489; and Frederick Bernays Wiener, "Courts-Martial and the Bill of Rights: The Original Practice," pt. I, *Harvard Law Review,* 72:7, 15–16 (Nov. 1958).

4. *Annals of Congress (The Debates and Proceedings in the Congress of the United States)* (Washington, 1834—), 8th Cong., 1st sess., p. 1123, March 8, 1804.

5. *Ibid.,* p. 1191, March 15, 1804.

6. *Ibid.*, 9th Cong., 1st sess., p. 1238.

7. Wiener, "Courts-Martial and the Bill of Rights," pt. II, *Harvard Law Review,* 72:268 (Dec. 1958).

8. Detlev F. Vagts, "Free Speech in the Armed Forces," *Columbia Law Review,* 57 (1957):192.

9. *Ibid.*, p. 190.

10. Willard Hurst, "Treason in the United States," *Harvard Law Review,* 58:248, 251, 267 (Dec. 1944); Boyd, I, 597, 598.

11. William Waller Hening, ed., *The Statutes at Large, Being a Collection of All the Laws of Virginia, 1619–1792* (Richmond, 1809–1823, 13 vols.), IX, 168 (Oct. 1776 sess., ch. III, "An Act Declaring What Shall Be Treason").

12. *Ibid.*, IX, 170–171 (Oct. 1776 sess., ch. V, "An Act for the Punishment of Certain Offenses").

13. *Ibid.,* X, 268–270 (May 1780 sess., ch. XIX, "An Act affixing Penalties to Certain Crimes"); Boyd, III, 493.

14. H. J. Eckenrode, *The Revolution in Virginia* (Boston, 1916), p. 242.

15. Jefferson to James Innes, May 2, 1781, Boyd, V, 593.

16. "A Tory has been properly defined to be a traitor in thought, but not in deed. The only description, by which the laws have endeavoured to come at them, was that of non-jurors, or persons refusing to take the oath of fidelity to the state." Jefferson, *Notes on the State of Virginia,* ed. by Peden, Query XVI, p. 155.

17. Quoted in Harold M. Hyman, *To Try Men's Souls: Loy-*

alty Tests in American History (Berkeley, Calif., 1959), p. 85, citing an undated manuscript fragment from the Jefferson Papers, no. 1003, Library of Congress. Professor Hyman generously provided me with a true copy of the fragment, which does not appear in the Boyd collection. The fragment includes the remark "General Washington's work against Tories best. Uses oaths well."

18. Hyman, *To Try Men's Souls,* p. 71.

19. Hening, ed., *Statutes of Virginia,* IX, 281–282 (May 1777 sess., "An Act to Oblige the Free Male Inhabitants of This State . . . to Give Assurance of Allegiance").

20. *Ibid.,* IX, 351.

21. *Ibid.,* IX, 549; Boyd, II, 219, 222.

22. *Ibid.,* X, 22–23; Boyd, II, 590. For an eloquent denunciation of such oaths, see *Historical Memoirs from 12 July 1776 to 25 July 1778 of William Smith,* ed. by William H. W. Sabine (New York, 1958), pp. 22, 410–412, 415.

23. Eckenrode, *Revolution in Virginia,* pp. 140–142, 184.

24. *Ibid.,* p. 185.

25. Hening, ed., *Statutes of Virginia,* IX, 373–374 (Oct. 1777 sess., ch. VI, "An Act for Indemnifying the Governour and Council . . . for Removing and Confining Suspected Persons during the Late Publick Danger"); Boyd, II, 119.

26. Hening, ed., *Statutes,* X, 309–315 (May 1780 sess., ch. XXXV, "An Act for Giving Farther Powers to the Governor and Council").

27. See Eckenrode, *Revolution in Virginia,* pp. 199, 206–214.

28. The same act vesting the governor with extraordinary powers authorized him to place the militia under martial law in order to keep them in service. Hening, ed., *Statutes,* X, 314; Boyd, III, 492, 497–498; and Eckenrode, *Revolution,* pp. 210–211, 214–220.

29. Eckenrode, pp. 243–244. Chapter 9 of Eckenrode is a good account of government measures against the "Spread of Disaffection." Eckenrode takes the position that the government under Jefferson tended to be quite lenient, even lax, in the enforcement of harsh laws against Tory offenders. Those who engaged in violence often received rough treatment, however, from the military. The terrorizing tactics of Colonel Charles Lynch, giving rise to the euphemism "lynch law," were not at all blameable on Governor Jefferson.

30. See Zechariah Chafee, Jr., *Three Human Rights in the Constitution of 1787* (Lawrence, Kan., 1956), pp. 90–161, for a history of bills of attainder in England. Chafee also edited a docu-

mentary history of bills of attainder in his *Documents on Fundamental Human Rights* (preliminary edition, published in three pamphlets) (Cambridge, Mass., 1952), Third Pamphlet, pp. 643–809.

31. *Rex v. Wilkes,* 4 Burrow (K.B.) 2527, 2545, 2559 (1770). There is no study of the use of the outlawry process in America. The colonial precedents are very few in number, indicating that outlawry never had more than a slight foothold in America. It was certainly a dying institution even in England, as Mansfield's opinion in the Wilkes case suggests. New York resorted to outlawry on a few occasions between 1702 and 1710, but not again thereafter. See Julius Goebel, Jr., and T. Raymond Naughton, *Law Enforcement in Colonial New York: A Study in Criminal Procedure, 1664–1776* (New York, 1944), pp. 442–445. In 1774 a New York act referred to the fact that outlawry "is not used in this Colony," but proclaiming the guilt of Ethan Allen and others for riot, required their surrender to the civil authorities on pain of being attainted for felony. Allen and his followers regarded the act as the equivalent of an outlawry and denounced it as unconstitutional. Goebel and Naughton, pp. 446–447. Pennsylvania's experience with outlawry provides an even more instructive contrast to that of Virginia. Under an act of 1718, one Aaron Doane was outlawed and attainted for robbery by the state supreme court in 1784 which sentenced him to be executed. However, the "President" of Pennsylvania withheld the warrant necessary to complete the sentence until he should receive from the court satisfactory answers to a series of questions revealing his implacable opposition to outlawry as a "menacing part of jurisprudence," "so dangerous a practice," and contrary to the "liberality of spirit" with which the laws should be enforced. The judges of the state supreme court, answering Dickinson's questions in detail, defended their use of outlawry. *Respublica v. Doane,* 1 Dallas 86–93 (1784). Dickinson and his council, however, rebuked the court for "establishing a precedent, in a capital case, altogether new . . . [and] so dangerous." Describing outlawry proceedings, even when controlled by the judiciary, as "vindictive supplements to a severe code of criminal jurisprudence," which would "weaken that security which the constitution appears to have intended for its citizens," Dickinson and the council refused to issue the warrant without which the sentence of death could not be carried out. "Proceedings of the Supreme Executive Council of Pennsylvania, in the case of the Commonwealth v. Doane," Appendix to 1 Dallas 495–498 (1795). Telford Taylor's *Grand Inquest: The*

Story of Congressional Investigations (New York, 1955), includes an appendix, pp. 301–305, with notes at pages 339–341, which gives a brief sketch on outlawry and useful references to early cases and writings on the subject.

32. Col. John Wilson to Gov. Patrick Henry, May 20, 1778, and Henry to Benjamin Harrison, speaker of the House of Delegates, May 27, 1778, in William Wirt, *Sketches of the Life and Character of Patrick Henry* (New York, 1832, 2 vols.), II, 235–238. For secondary accounts, see W. P. Trent, "The Case of Josiah Philips," *American Historical Review,* I (1896): 444–454, and Jesse Turner, "A Phantom Precedent," *American Law Review,* 48:321–344 (May, June 1914).

33. Jefferson to William Wirt, Aug. 14, 1814, in Lipscomb, XIV, 170.

34. The bill of attainder and outlawry is in Hening, ed., *Statutes,* IX, 463–464 (May 1778 sess., "Bill to Attaint Josiah Philips and Others"); Boyd, II, 189–191.

35. Copies of the indictment, the trial minutes, the sentence of the court, and notice of the execution are in Wirt, *Henry,* vol. II, app. note C, pp. 17–19.

36. Jefferson to Wirt, Aug. 14, 1814, in Lipscomb, XIV, 170. See also Jefferson to L. H. Girardin, March 12, 1815, in *ibid.,* pp. 277–278.

37. Article 8 stated: "That in all capital or criminal prosecutions a man hath a right to . . . be confronted with the accusers and witnesses, to call for evidence in his favour, and to a speedy trial by an impartial jury of twelve men of his vicinage, without whose unanimous consent he cannot be found guilty . . . that no man be deprived of his liberty, except by the law of the land or the judgment of his peers." Virginia Constitution of 1776, in Francis Newton Thorpe, ed., *The Federal and State Constitutions, Colonial Charters, and Other Organic Laws of the . . . United States* (Washington, 1909, 7 vols.), VII, 3813.

38. Jefferson himself remembered that Philips had been executed after receiving due process of law, but thought that there had been no proceeding on the bill of attainder as a result of Randolph's generous waiver of the government's right under that bill. That Philips was captured before the attainder had gone into operation was forgotten or unknown until the publication of Jesse Turner's research in 1914; see "A Phantom Precedent," *American Law Review,* 48:3.

39. Quoted in Jonathan Elliot, ed., *The Debates in the Several State Conventions on the Adoption of the Federal Con-*

stitution . . . and Other Illustrations of the Constitution (Philadelphia, 1941, reprinting the 2nd rev. ed. of 5 vols. in 2), III, 66–67.

40. *Ibid.*, III, 193.

41. *Ibid.*, III, 140.

42. *Ibid.*, III, 223. See also speeches of Nicholas (III, 236, 450), Pendleton (III, 299), and Randolph (III, 193).

43. Jefferson to Girardin, March 12, 1815, in Lipscomb, XIV, 271–278.

44. *Ibid.*, XIV, 277.

45. Jefferson to Wirt, May 12, 1815, in Paul Leicester Ford, ed., *The Writings of Thomas Jefferson* (New York, 1892–1899, 10 vols.), IX, 472. Hereafter cited as Ford.

46. "Jefferson's Draft of a Constitution for Virginia," May–June, 1783, in Boyd, VI, 298. The quoted parenthetical words were not included in the final draft.

THREE. A FEW WHOLESOME PROSECUTIONS: THE PROBLEM OF A FREE PRESS

1. Sometime after May 15, 1776, and before June 13, 1776, Jefferson composed three drafts of a constitution for Virginia. They are printed in Boyd, I, 337–364.

2. Boyd, I, 344.

3. *Ibid.*, 353.

4. "A Bill for Establishing Religious Freedom," in *ibid.*, II, 546. This bill was presented to the Virginia legislature in 1779 and adopted in 1785; the text, as adopted, is in Hening, ed., *Statutes*, XII, 84–86. Furneaux's ideas on religious liberty were published in his *Letters to the Honourable Mr. Justice Blackstone, Concerning His Exposition of the Act of Toleration . . . in His Celebrated Commentaries on the Laws of England* (London, 1770). I have used the second edition, London, 1771, in which, at pages 59–63, the passages that influenced Jefferson appear. There were two American editions of Furneaux, both published in 1773 in Philadelphia, both reprintings of the London edition of 1771, under the titles *An Interesting Appendix to Sir William Blackstone's Commentaries on the Laws of England* and *The Palladium of Conscience*. For a discussion of Furneaux and the overt-acts test, see Leonard W. Levy, *Legacy of Suppression: Freedom of Speech and Press in Early American History* (Cambridge, Mass., 1960), pp. 164–169. Furneaux's views also received circulation in the writings of Ebenezer Ratcliffe, *Two Letters Addressed to the*

Right Rev. Prelates (London, 1773), and Andrew Kippis, *A Vindication of the Protestant Dissenting Ministers* (London, 1773), both discussed in Levy, *Legacy*, pp. 169–170.

5. *Notes on Virginia*, ed. by Peden, p. 159.

6. *A Fragment on Government* (London, 1776), p. 154.

7. *An Enquiry into the Extent of the Power of Juries, on Trials of Indictments or Informations, for Publishing Seditious, or Other Criminal Writings. Extracted from a Miscellaneous Collection of Papers That Were Published in 1776, Intitled, Additional Papers Concerning the Province of Quebec* (Dublin, 1792), pp. 6, 13, 18, 22, 24, 28.

8. *The Deformity of the Doctrine of Libels, and Informations Ex Officio* (London, 1785), pp. 11–24, 28. For a discussion of the origins of the overt-acts test, see Levy, *Legacy*, pp. 153–157, 164–175, 251–257.

9. Boyd, VI, 304. A documentary history of "Jefferson's Proposed Revision of the Virginia Constitution," preceded by an elaborate editorial introduction, is in Boyd, VI, 278f.

10. Article 12, Virginia Constitution of 1776, in Thorpe, ed., *Federal and State Constitutions*, VII, 3814.

11. Boyd, VI, 288. Jefferson had the Albemarle proposals before him when composing his 1783 revision of the Virginia constitution. *Ibid.*, 282.

12. *Rex v. Zenger* (1735) in Thomas B. Howell, ed., *A Complete Collection of State Trials to 1783* (London, 1816–1828, 34 vols.), XVII, 675. See also Livingston Rutherfurd, *John Peter Zenger, His Press, His Trial and a Bibliography of Zenger Imprints. Also a Reprint of the First Edition of the Trial* (New York, 1904), pp. 198, 206, 207, 209, 212, 216, 223, 240.

13. See Levy, *Legacy*, for discussion of truth as a defense.

14. See *ibid.* for discussion of the jury question.

15. Jefferson to Munroe, May 5, 1811, in Lipscomb, XIII, 59.

16. Jefferson to John Norvell, June 11, 1807, in Lipscomb, XI, 224.

17. Jefferson to Madison, July 31, 1788, in Boyd, XIII, 442–443.

18. On the English or common-law definition of freedom of the press as the absence of prior restraints, and its acceptance in the United States, see Levy, *Legacy*.

19. *Annals of Congress*, 1st Cong., 1st sess., 451.

20. Jefferson to Madison, Aug. 28, 1789, in Boyd, XV, 367.

21. Quoted in Bradford Perkins, *The First Rapprochement: England and the United States, 1795–1805* (Philadelphia, 1955),

pp. 33–34, citing Jefferson to Madison, Aug. 3, 1795, Madison MSS, vol. XVIII, Library of Congress.

22. The description of Jefferson writing "with some glee" is taken from Perkins, *First Rapprochement,* p. 34.

23. See Adrienne Koch, *Jefferson and Madison: The Great Collaboration* (New York, 1950), ch. 7, "The Virginia and Kentucky Resolutions: In Defense of Civil Liberties," pp. 174–211.

24. For a detailed discussion of "The Emergence of an American Libertarian Theory," see Levy, *Legacy,* ch. 6.

25. *The Virginia Report of 1799–1800* (Richmond, 1850), p. 220. *The Virginia Report* originally appeared as a tract of over eighty pages. The copy in the Langdell Treasure Room, Harvard Law Library, is bound together with the 1799 issue of Hay's *Essay,* cited in the next note. Madison wrote the *Report* at the close of 1799; it was adopted by the Virginia legislature on Jan. 11, 1800, which immediately published it. It is reproduced in Elliot, ed., *Debates,* IV, 546–80, under the title, "Madison's Report on the Virginia Resolutions . . . Report of the Committee to Whom Were Referred the Communications of Various States, Relative to the Resolutions of the Last General Assembly of This State, Concerning the Alien and Sedition Laws." The *Report* is also available in Gaillard Hunt, ed., *The Writings of James Madison* (New York, 1900–1910, 9 vols.), VI, 341–406. The full title of the edition cited here is *The Virginia Report of 1799–1800, Touching the Alien and Sedition Laws; Together with the Virginia Resolutions of December 21, 1798, The Debates and Proceedings Thereon, in the House of Delegates in Virginia* (Richmond, 1850), pp. 189–237, a book of great value for its inclusion of the Virginia debates on the Sedition Act, at pp. 22–161. Those debates added little to the debates of the House of Representatives, but the remarks of Republican speakers constitute another example of the new libertarianism.

26. ("Hortensius"), *An Essay on the Liberty of the Press. Respectfully Inscribed to the Republican Printers throughout the United States* (Richmond, 1803, reprinting the text of the first edition, Philadelphia, 1799), p. 29. See also Hay's other tract with a similar title, *An Essay on the Liberty of the Press, Shewing, That the Requisition of Security for Good Behavior from Libellers, is Perfectly Compatible with the Constitution and Laws of Virginia* (Richmond, 1803), p. 32. This latter tract will be hereafter cited as the 1803 tract; the former one as the 1803 ed. of the 1799 tract.

27. *An Enquiry, Concerning the Liberty, and Licentiousness of the Press* (New York, 1801), pp. 6–7.

28. *Virginia Report of 1799–1800,* pp. 226–227.

29. *A Treatise Concerning Political Enquiry, and the Liberty of the Press* (New York, 1800), p. 253. Wortman, one of the leading democratic theoreticians of his time, was a New York lawyer prominent in Tammany politics. From 1801–1807 he served as clerk of the City and County of New York. He was the author of several important tracts, one of which outlined a democratic philosophy of social reform, *An Oration on the Influence of Social Institutions upon Human Morals and Happiness* (New York, 1796), 31 pp., and another which was a leading defense of Jefferson against charges of atheism in the election of 1800. See *A Solemn Address, to Christians and Patriots upon the Approaching Election of a President of the United States* (New York, 1800), 36 pp. Gallatin supported the publication of Wortman's *Enquiry* by undertaking to secure subscriptions to the book among Republican members of Congress. Wortman to Gallatin, MS letters, Dec. 24 and Dec. 30, 1799, Gallatin Papers, 1799, nos. 47 and 49, New York Historical Society. In 1813–14 Wortman published a newspaper in New York, the *Standard of Union,* to which Jefferson subscribed in the hope that it would counteract the "abandoned spirit of falsehood" of the newspapers of the country. Jefferson to Wortman, MS letter, Aug. 15, 1813, Jefferson Papers, Henry E. Huntington Library.

30. *Essay on the Liberty of the Press* (1803 ed. of 1799 tract), p. 28.

31. *Annals of Congress,* 5th Cong., 2nd sess., 2162.

32. *Enquiry, Concerning Liberty,* p. 68.

33. *Virginia Report of 1799–1800,* p. 226.

34. *Treatise Concerning Political Enquiry,* p. 262.

35. *Essay on the Liberty of the Press* (1803 ed. of 1799 tract), pp. 23–24.

36. *Ibid.,* p. 25.

37. *Essay on the Liberty of the Press* (1803 tract), p. 29.

38. Wortman, *Treatise,* pp. 140, 253; Thomson, *Enquiry,* p. 79.

39. *Enquiry, Concerning the Liberty, and Licentiousness of the Press,* p. 22.

40. *Virginia Report of 1799–1800,* p. 220.

41. *Treatise Concerning Political Enquiry,* p. 29.

42. Thomson, *Enquiry,* pp. 20, 22; Hay, *Essay* (1803 ed. of 1799 tract), p. 26.

43. "Originality" refers to the American scene. American libertarian thought lagged behind its British counterpart which very likely provided a model for the Republicans in the same way that British thought advocating suppression influenced Federalist opinion. For British precursors of the new American libertarianism, see Levy, *Legacy,* pp. 91–125, 137–175, 249–257.

44. Kentucky Resolutions of 1798, in Elliot, ed., *Debates,* IV, 540–541.

45. Undated memorandum of 1801, intended as a message to the Senate, in Ford, VIII, 56.

46. Jefferson to Livingston, May 31, 1801, in Ford, VIII, 56.

47. Jefferson to Gallatin, Nov. 12, 1801, in Ford, VIII, 57.

48. Jefferson to Levi Lincoln, March 24, 1802, in Ford, VIII, 139.

49. Jefferson to Monsieur Pictet, Feb. 5, 1803, in Lipscomb, X, 357.

50. Jefferson to McKean, Feb. 19, 1803, in Ford, VIII, 218–219.

51. *Respublica v. Dennie,* 4 Yeates' (Penn.) Reports 267 (1805).

52. *People v. Croswell,* 3 Johnson's (N.Y.) Cases 336 (1804).

53. Article signed "Fair Play," sent to Levi Lincoln for anonymous transmittal to the press, June 1, 1803, in Ford, VIII, 238.

54. Jefferson to Abigail Adams, Sept. 11, 1804, in Lipscomb, XI, 51–52. Jefferson apparently used the word "slander" in a generic sense. He could not have literally meant slander, which technically applies to spoken defamation, since he was referring to the press. More significantly, the subject of discussion between Jefferson and Mrs. Adams was the publication of opinions made criminal by the Sedition Act.

55. Second Inaugural Address, March 4, 1805, in Ford, VIII, 346.

56. "Hampden," *A Letter to the President of the United States Touching the Prosecutions under His Patronage, before the Circuit Court in the District of Connecticut* (New Haven, 1808), p. 28.

57. The Litchfield (Conn.) *Witness,* April 30, 1806, as quoted by William A. Robinson in his sketch of Edwards in the *Dictionary of American Biography.*

58. "Hampden," *A Letter to the President,* pp. 8–12.

59. Jefferson to Wilson C. Nicholas, June 13, 1809, in Lipscomb, XII, 289. Italics added.

60. "From the Citizens of Hartford," Seymour and others to Jefferson, in Worthington C. Ford, ed., *Thomas Jefferson. Correspondence Printed from the Originals in the Collections of William K. Bixby* (Boston, 1916), pp. 137, 139.

61. *Annals of Congress,* 9th Cong., 2nd sess., 247.

62. Jefferson to Seymour, Feb. 11, 1807, in Lipscomb, XI, 155.

63. "Hampden," *A Letter to the President,* p. iii.

64. When Brockholst Livingston was appointed by Jefferson to succeed Justice Paterson, he was inexplicably not assigned to circuit duty for a year, leaving Edwards to preside alone. Livingston, as a member of the high court of New York had joined Chief Justice Morgan Lewis' opinion, in *People v. Croswell,* that the English common law of seditious libel, as laid down by Lord Mansfield and Blackstone, prevailed in the state of New York. *People v. Croswell,* 3 Johnson's (N.Y.) Cases 336, 337–339, 394–411 (1804).

65. "Hampden," *A Letter to the President,* p. 20.

66. *Ibid.,* pp. 14–16.

67. *Ibid.,* p. 20.

68. *Ibid.,* p. 19.

69. *Ibid.,* pp. 19–23.

70. Jefferson to Nicholas, June 13, 1809, in Lipscomb, XII, 288. Jefferson's letter to Nicholas is as follows: "I had observed in a newspaper, (some years ago, I do not recollect the time exactly,) some dark hints of a prosecution in Connecticut, but so obscurely hinted that I paid little attention to it. Some considerable time after, it was again mentioned, so that I understood that some prosecution was going on in the federal court there, for calumnies uttered from the pulpit against me by a clergyman. I immediately wrote to Mr. Granger, who, I think, was in Connecticut at the time, stating that I had laid it down as a law to myself, to take no notice of the thousand calumnies issued against me, but to trust my character to my own conduct, and the good sense and candor of my fellow citizens; that I had found no reason to be dissatisfied with that course, and I was unwilling it should be broke through by others as to any matter concerning me; and I therefore requested him to desire the district attorney to dismiss the prosecution. Some time after this, I heard of subpoenas being served on General Lee, David M. Randolph, and others, as witnesses to attend the trial. I then for the first time conjectured the subject of the libel. I immediately wrote to Mr. Granger, to require an immediate dismission of the prosecution. The answer of Mr. Huntington, the district attorney, was, that these subpoenas had been issued by the defendant without his knowledge, that it had been his intention to dismiss all the prosecutions at the first meeting of the court, and to accompany it with an avowal of his opinion, that they could not be maintained, because the federal

court had no jurisdiction over libels. This was accordingly done. I did not till then know that there were other prosecutions of the same nature, nor do I now know what were their subjects. But all went off together; and I afterwards saw in the hands of Mr. Granger, a letter written by the clergyman, disavowing any personal ill will towards me, and solemnly declaring he had never uttered the words charged. I think Mr. Granger either showed me, or said there were affidavits of at least half a dozen respectable men, who were present at the sermon and swore no such expressions were uttered, and as many equally respectable who swore the contrary. But the clergyman expressed his gratification at the dismission of the prosecution. I write all this from memory, and after too long an interval of time to be certain of the exactness of all the details; but I am sure there is no variation material, and Mr. Granger, correcting small lapses of memory, can confirm every thing substantial. Certain it is, that the prosecutions had been instituted, and had made considerable progress, without my knowledge, that they were disapproved by me as soon as known, and directed to be discontinued. The attorney did it on the same ground on which I had acted myself in the cases of Duane, Callendar and others; to wit, that the sedition law was unconstitutional and null, and that my obligation to execute what was law, involved that of not suffering rights secured by valid laws, to be prostrated by what was no law. I always understood that these prosecutions had been invited, if not instituted, by Judge Edwards, and the marshal being republican, had summoned a grand jury partly or wholly republican; but that Mr. Huntington declared from the beginning against the jurisdiction of the court, and had determined to enter *nolle prosequis* before he received my directions." Note Jefferson's claim that he had first told Granger to dismiss the suit against Backus at an unspecified early date before he had learned the nature of the minister's libel. Note also his claim that he did not know that there were other prosecutions until his second command to dismiss the suit. But the letter from Seymour and the President's response, more than two years before the letter to Nicholas, conclusively disprove his statements; so, inferentially, does the conduct of Judge Edwards at the April 1807 session of the court, two months after Jefferson's letter to Seymour. It was not until the September session that Edwards sought to put an end to the trials. As for Jefferson's statement that Huntington, the district attorney, intended to dismiss the prosecutions at the first meeting of the court, which would have been in April 1807, the facts are that fresh indictments were drawn at that time against Backus, Hudson, and Goodwin, after the original indictments were shown to have had defects. "Hampden," *A Letter to the President,* p. 15.

71. Jefferson to Robert Smith, July 1, 1805, quoted in Dumas Malone, *Jefferson the Virginian,* p. 448. See Malone, pp. 447–451, for a discussion of the Walker affair.

72. Among the Supreme Court justices who accepted jurisdiction of common-law crimes, in circuit court cases, were Wilson, Ellsworth, Paterson, Jay, Iredell, and Chase. For cases of the first decade of the court's work, see, "Trial of Joseph Ravara" (1792), in Francis Wharton, ed., *State Trials of the United States during the Administrations of Washington and Adams* (Philadelphia, 1849), pp. 90–92; "Trial of Gideon Henfield" (1793), in *ibid.,* pp. 49–92; *U.S. v. Worrall,* 2 Dallas 384 (1798) in *ibid.,* pp. 188–199; "Trial of the Northampton Insurgents" (1799), in *ibid.,* p. 476; "Trial of Isaac Williams" (1799), in *ibid.,* pp. 652–654. See also *U.S. v. Smith* (1797), MS, Final Record of the United States Circuit Courts of Massachusetts, 1790–1799, I, 242, 244 (Federal Records Center, Dorchester, Mass.). Smith's case is reported in 27 *Federal Cases* 1147–1148, case no. 16,323, where the date is erroneously given as 1792. Justice Chase in Worrall's case, mentioned above, disagreed with his associate Judge Peters who supported the jurisdiction of the federal courts in cases of common-law crime. Chase, however, changed his opinion in *U.S. v. Sylvester* (1799), MS, Final Record, I, 303, an unreported case.

73. *U.S. v. Hudson and Goodwin,* 7 Cranch (U.S.) 32 (1812). W. W. Crosskey, *Politics and the Constitution* (Chicago, 1953, 2 vols.), II, 782, states that Chief Justice Marshall and Justices Story and Washington dissented from Johnson's opinion without noting the fact of their dissent on the record. That the court was divided was clear from the fact that Story made his dissent known in a circuit decision of the following year, *U.S. v. Coolidge,* 1 Gallison 488 (1813), and from the statement of Johnson, noting the division of the court, in *U.S. v. Coolidge,* 1 Wheaton (U.S.) 415 (1816).

74. Jefferson to Edward Carrington, Jan. 16, 1787, in Boyd, XI, 49.

75. Jefferson to John Norvell, June 11, 1807, in Lipscomb, XI, 224.

76. Jefferson to Walter Jones, Jan. 2, 1814, in Lipscomb, XIV, 46. To Tunis Wortman, a year earlier, Jefferson stated that the

press was so given to falsehoods, even truth itself became suspect if published in a newspaper. To Wortman, MS letter, Aug. 15, 1813, Jefferson Papers, Henry E. Huntington Library.

77. Jefferson to Nathaniel Macon, Jan. 12, 1819, in Lipscomb, XV, 179.

78. See Jefferson to Monroe, June 11, 1823, in Lipscomb, XV, 435.

79. Jefferson to Monsieur A. Coray, Oct. 31, 1823, in Lipscomb, XV, 489.

80. For a very different interpretation of the subject of this chapter, see Frank L. Mott, *Jefferson and the Press* (Baton Rouge, La., 1943).

FOUR. A DICTATORSHIP IN EXTREME CASES: THE BURR CONSPIRACY

1. Special Message to Congress on Burr, Jan. 22, 1807, in Ford, IX, 14–20. The account of the Burr conspiracy and trials in this chapter is based on standard studies, among them, Walter Flavius McCaleb, *The Aaron Burr Conspiracy* (New York, 1936); Thomas Perkins Abernethy, *The Burr Conspiracy* (New York, 1954); Nathan Schachner, *Aaron Burr, A Biography* (New York, 1937); Albert J. Beveridge, *The Life of John Marshall* (Boston, 1919, 4 vols.), vol. III; and Henry Adams, *History of the United States during the Administrations of Thomas Jefferson and James Madison* (New York, 1889–1891, 9 vols.), vol. III.

2. Adams to Benjamin Rush, Feb. 2, 1807, quoted in Beveridge, *Life of John Marshall,* III, 338, citing *Old Family Letters,* 128–129. At Burr's trial, Edmund Randolph of defense counsel declared, "The president's declaration of Burr's guilt is unconstitutional." Randolph explained that Jefferson had made himself both accuser and judge in the case, although he had no right to give opinions on the guilt of any person and had prejudiced Burr's chance for a fair trial. David Robertson, ed., *Reports of the Trials of Colonel Aaron Burr . . . for Treason, and for a Misdemeanor . . . in the Circuit Court of the United States* (Philadelphia, 1808, 2 vols.), I, 159–160. See also the similar comment by Luther Martin, who also defended Burr, in *ibid.,* I, 128.

3. See the extraordinary series of letters from Jefferson to George Hay, between May and September, 1807, in Ford, IX, 52–63, where they are conveniently located together.

4. To James Bowdoin, the American ambassador in Madrid, Jefferson wrote, in the midst of the prosecution of Burr, that "Never did a nation act towards another with more perfidy and injustice than Spain has constantly practised against us. And if

we have kept our hands off her till now, it has been purely out of respect for France, & from the value we set on the friendship of France. We expect therefore from the friendship of the emperor that he will either compel Spain to do us justice, or abandon her to us. We ask but one month to be in possession of the city of Mexico." Jefferson to Bowdoin, April 2, 1807, in Ford, IX, 40–41. At Burr's trial, his counsel quoted public statements by the President to prove that a war with Spain would have been meritorious. *Trials of Burr,* I, 5.

5. Jefferson to Bollman, Jan. 25, 1807, in Matthew L. Davis, *Memoirs of Aaron Burr* (New York, 1837, 2 vols.), II, 388. The words quoted are allegedly Jefferson's; the italics were probably added by Davis or Bollman.

6. *Ex Parte Bollman* and *Ex Parte Swartwout,* 4 Cranch (U.S.) 75 (1807).

7. Jefferson to Hay, May 20, 1807, in Lipscomb, XI, 205.

8. Jefferson to Hay, May 28, 1807, *ibid.,* XI, 210.

9. Trials of Burr, I, 190–196, *passim.*

10. Jefferson to Hay, June 19, 1807, in Lipscomb, XI, 233.

11. *Ibid.,* pp. 234–235.

12. *Trials of Burr,* I, 39–43.

13. *Ibid.,* pp. 38–39.

14. Jefferson to Hay, May 26, 1807, in Lipscomb, XI, 209.

15. Jefferson to John W. Eppes, May 28, 1807, in Ford, IX, 68.

16. Jackson to W. Patten Anderson, June 16, 1807, quoted in James Parton, *Life of Andrew Jackson* (New York, 1861, 3 vols.), I, 335.

17. *Trials of Burr,* I, 44, 46.

18. Jefferson to Giles, April 20, 1807, in Lipscomb, XI, 187.

19. *Trials of Burr,* I, 13–18.

20. Jefferson to Bowdoin, April 2, 1807, in Lipscomb, XI, 186.

21. Jefferson to Giles, April 20, 1807, in Lipscomb, XI, 190.

22. Beveridge, *Life of Marshall,* III, 303–305, 344–345; Schachner, *Aaron Burr,* pp. 314–316.

23. Jefferson to John Norvell, June 11, 1807, in Lipscomb, XI, 224–225.

24. McCaleb, *Burr Conspiracy,* p. 228.

25. *Annals of Congress,* 10th Cong., 1st sess., "Trial of Aaron Burr," testimony of Wilkinson and Dinsmore, pp. 528–530, 536–537, 661. See also McCaleb, *Burr Conspiracy,* pp. 229–232. Trial testimony is more fully reported in the *Annals of Congress* than in Robertson's *Trials of Burr* which is more valuable for arguments of counsel and judicial rulings.

26. Jefferson to Madison, March 15, 1789, in Boyd, XIV, 659.

27. Jefferson to Giles, April 20, 1807, in Lipscomb, XI, 191. In Ford's edition the word "immunity" is given as "impunity." Ford, IX, 46.

28. Jefferson to Eppes, May 28, 1807, in Ford, IX, 68. The grand jury included fourteen Republicans out of sixteen members, but four were "Quids" or Randolph Republicans.

29. Jefferson to Wilkinson, Sept. 20, 1807, in Lipscomb, XI, 375. See also Jefferson to William Thomson, Sept. 26, 1807, in Ford, IX, 143–144.

30. Seventh Annual Message, Oct. 27, 1807, in Ford, IX, 163–164; also, *Annals of Congress,* 10th Cong., 1st sess., p. 18.

31. *Annals of Congress,* 8th Cong., 2nd sess., p. 1213; 9th Cong., 1st sess., pp. 446, 499–507.

32. *Annals of Congress,* 10th Cong., 1st sess., pp. 21–22, 99.

33. McCaleb, *Burr Conspiracy,* p. 145. After Burr's trial, Wilkinson submitted a bill to Spain for $200,000 in connection with his services in defeating Burr's plan to invade Mexico. Davis, *Memoirs of Burr,* II, 400–404.

34. Wilkinson to Claiborne, Dec. 7, 1806, quoted in McCaleb, *Burr Conspiracy,* p. 145.

35. Quoted in McCaleb, *Burr Conspiracy,* p. 183. For a slightly variant form of Wilkinson's reply, see *Annals of Congress,* 9th Cong., 2nd sess., pp. 530–531.

36. Quoted in McCaleb, *Burr Conspiracy,* pp. 184–185.

37. On Wilkinson's exploits, see *ibid.,* ch. 8 and pp. 235–237.

38. Jefferson to Wilkinson, Feb. 3, 1807, in Lipscomb, XI, 148–149.

39. *Ibid.,* p. 150.

40. Jefferson to Claiborne, Feb. 3, 1807, in Lipscomb, XI, 151.

41. Special Message to Congress, Jan. 22, 1807, in Ford, IX, 20.

42. *Annals of Congress,* 9th Cong., 2nd sess., pp. 44, 402. The only account of the Senate's secret debates is in the journal of Senator William Plumer of New Hampshire which is an invaluable source for the Burr conspiracy as events were seen from Washington by a reliable reporter, close to the President, who knew or interviewed most of the participants, including Bollman, Swartwout, Adair, and others. Plumer's observations on Burr, Wilkinson, and Eaton are especially interesting and perceptive. For his account of the Senate debate on the habeas corpus bill, see Everett Somerville Brown, ed., *William Plumer's Memorandum of Proceedings in the United States Senate, 1803–1807* (New York, 1923), pp. 585–589.

43. *Annals of Congress,* 9th Cong., 2nd sess., pp. 402–425.

44. *Plumer's Memorandum,* p. 590.

45. *Ibid.,* pp. 585, 590. Sen. Giles who introduced the bill was the Administration's principal spokesman in the Senate, Jefferson's closest political lieutenant. On the other hand, Jefferson's son-in-law, Congressman Eppes, was one of the most vigorous opponents of the bill in the House. It is most unlikely, therefore, that the bill originated in the White House. It is unquestionable, however, that if the bill had passed the House it would have been signed into law. The opposition in the House was apparently unexpected. It was, in part, based on resentment against the Senate's highhanded methods of presentation.

46. *Annals of Congress,* 9th Cong., 2nd sess., p. 472.

47. *Ibid.,* pp. 502–590.

48. Quoted in McCaleb, *Burr Conspiracy,* p. 198.

49. Jefferson to Gaines, July 23, 1807, in Lipscomb, XI, 293.

50. Jefferson to Wilkinson, June 21, 1807, in Lipscomb, XI, 249. For a contrasting view, suggesting that the President had lost touch with public opinion, see *Plumer's Memorandum* for 1807. As early as Feb. 21, Plumer, noting that Adair, Alexander, Bollman, Ogden, and Swartwout, all victims of Wilkinson's New Orleans "fiery trial," had been found innocent, entered the following observations in his *Memorandum:* "But this vain intriguing haughty infamous Wilkinson, deprived them of the rights which our laws guarantee even to common *convicted* malefactors . . . Wilkinson has done more to destroy our little feeble military establishment, than its bitterest enemies have been able for years to effect. The President ought instantly to remove him from his two offices of Gov of Upper Louisiana & commander of the army. If he does not do it, Wilkinson will damn him & his administration. Thomas M. Randolph told me he tho't Wilkinson must be removed or his father in law [Jefferson's] administration would fall. The public indignation seems now to be transferred from Burr to Wilkinson . . . It is now very apparent Wilkinson himself has *created* much of the alarm, & has greatly exaggerated the force & importance of Burr." *Plumer's Memorandum,* pp. 618–619.

51. In Bollman's case, for example, Chief Justice Marshall declared: "It would, too, be extremely dangerous to say, that because the prisoners were apprehended, not by a civil magistrate, but by the military power, there could be given by law a right to try the persons so seized in any place which the general might select, and to which he might direct them to be carried." *Ex parte Bollman,* 4 Cranch (U.S.) 75, 136 (1807).

52. Jefferson to James Brown, Oct. 27, 1808, in Lipscomb, XII, 183.

53. *Plumer's Memorandum,* p. 619.

54. *Annals of Congress,* 9th Cong., 2nd sess., p. 537.

55. *Ibid.,* pp. 532–533.

56. Boyd, VI, 84–86, 88, 91; Malone, *Jefferson the Virginian,* p. 361.

57. Jefferson, *Notes on Virginia,* Peden, ed., pp. 126–129.

58. Jefferson to John B. Colvin, Sept. 20, 1810, in Lipscomb, XII, 418–421.

FIVE. PASSIVE RESISTANCE ENFORCED BY BAYONETS: THE EMBARGO, I

1. In a letter to Robert R. Livingston, Jefferson described the French capture of American vessels on the high seas as "piracy." However, the general tone of the letter was, strangely enough, a friendly one toward Napoleon. The Emperor, wrote Jefferson, "does not wish us to go to war with England, knowing we have no ships to carry on that war. To submit to pay to England the tribute on our commerce which she demands by her orders of council, would be to aid her in the war against him, and would give him just grounds to declare war with us. He concludes, therefore, as every rational man must, that the embargo, the only remaining alternative, was a wise measure. These are acknowledged principles, and should circumstances arise which may offer advantage to our country in making them public, we shall avail ourselves of them." To Livingston, Oct. 15, 1808, in Lipscomb, XII, 170. With ideas such as these, indicating that Federalist charges were not wholly baseless, it was best that Jefferson spoke not at all, for only an expression of sentiments contrary to those of the letter (excepting the remark about piracy) would have served the public interest.

2. Dec. 8, 1801, in Ford, VIII, 124–125.

3. Gallatin to Jefferson, Dec. 18, 1807, in Henry Adams, ed., *The Writings of Albert Gallatin* (Philadelphia, 1879, 3 vols.), I, 368.

4. *Annals of Congress,* 10th Cong., 1st sess., p. 50.

5. *Ibid.,* app. pp. 2327–2330.

6. *Ibid.,* p. 50.

7. *Ibid.,* pp. 1216–1222.

8. *Ibid.,* pp. 2815–2817.

9. *Ibid.,* pp. 78, 1271.

10. *Ibid.,* pp. 104, 2337–2342, Feb. 4, 1807.

11. *Ibid.,* pp. 2839–2842.

12. *Ibid.,* pp. 160–161.
13. *Ibid.,* pp. 1653–1657, Feb. 20, 1807.
14. *Ibid.,* pp. 1710–1712.
15. *Ibid.,* pp. 170–171, March 17, 1808.
16. See "Replies to Public Addresses," in Lipscomb, XVI, 301–345, *passim.*
17. Gallatin to Jefferson, Aug. 9 and Aug. 17, 1808, in *Writings of Gallatin,* I, 403–404, 406.
18. Jefferson to the Legislature of N.H., Aug. 2, 1808, in Lipscomb, XVI, 308.
19. Louis Martin Sears, *Jefferson and the Embargo* (Durham, N.C., 1927), p. 105.
20. "To the Inhabitants of the Towns of Boston, Newburyport and Providence, in Legal Town Meeting Assembled," Aug. 26, 1808, in Lipscomb, XVI, 312–314.
21. Act of April 25, 1808, *Annals of Congress,* 10th Cong., 1st sess., pp. 2870–2874.
22. *Ibid.,* pp. 371–372.
23. *Ibid.,* pp. 2263–2268.
24. Gallatin to Jefferson, July 29, 1808, in *Writings of Gallatin,* I, 398.
25. *Annals of Congress,* 10th Cong., 2nd sess., p. 12; Ford, IX, 220.
26. See letters of Jefferson to Gallatin, Dec. 24, 1807, Jan. 7, March 31, and April 2, 1808, in Lipscomb, XI, 407, 415; XII, 24–25, 26–27. See also the letters of Jefferson to Gallatin, March 30, April 2, and Oct. 25, 1808, in *Writings of Gallatin,* I, 379–380, 383, and 420.
27. Jefferson to Gallatin, May 6, 1808, in *Writings of Gallatin,* I, 386. Ten days later Jefferson wrote, "In order to give this law the effect intended, we find it necessary to consider every vessel as suspicious which has on board any articles of domestic produce in demand at foreign markets, and most especially provisions." To Gallatin, May 16, 1808, in *ibid.,* p. 389.
28. Jefferson to Gallatin, March 30, 1808, in *ibid.,* p. 380.
29. Gallatin to Jefferson, April 1, 1808, in *ibid.,* p. 382.
30. Gallatin to Jefferson, July 29, 1808, in *ibid.,* p. 396.
31. Jefferson to Gallatin, Nov. 13, 1808, in Lipscomb, XII, 194.
32. Jefferson to Levi Lincoln, Nov. 13, 1808, in *ibid.,* XII, 194.
33. *Annals of Congress,* 10th Cong., 2nd sess., pp. 580–581. The proclamation was not announced until the following month, after the marshal's posse had failed to suppress the insurrection. See Jefferson to Gallatin, April 19, 1808, in Lipscomb, XII, 30–31;

Adams, *History of the U.S.*, IV, 249; Bennett Milton Rich, *The Presidents and Civil Disorder* (Washington, 1941), p. 32; and Walter Wilson Jennings, *The American Embargo, 1807–1809* (Iowa City, 1921), p. 113.

34. Quoted in Rich, *Presidents and Civil Disorder*, p. 32.

35. Jefferson to William Stephens Smith, Nov. 13, 1787, in Boyd, XII, 356.

36. Jefferson to Uriah Forrest, Dec. 31, 1787, in *ibid.*, 442–443, 478.

37. Edward S. Corwin, *The President: Office and Powers* (New York, 1948), p. 161.

38. *Annals of Congress*, 9th Cong., 2nd sess., p. 1286, Act of March 3, 1807.

39. First Annual Message, Dec. 8, 1801, in Ford, VIII, 121.

40. Ford, VIII, 495.

41. *Annals of Congress*, 10th Cong., 1st sess., pp. 1514–1515, Jan. 27, 1808.

42. *Ibid.*, pp. 1631, 1638, Feb. 17, 1808.

43. *Ibid.*, pp. 1690–1691, Feb. 26, 1808.

44. See speeches of Randolph of Virginia and Stanford of North Carolina in *ibid.*, pp. 1904–1912, 1939–1952, 1959–1973.

45. *Ibid.*, p. 2062. The Senate vote was unrecorded. See *ibid.*, p. 378.

46. Act of March 30, 1808, in *ibid.*, p. 2846.

47. Act of Dec. 22, 1807, in *ibid.*, pp. 2814–2815.

48. Jefferson to Gallatin, Dec. 24, 1807, in Lipscomb, XI, 407.

49. Jefferson to Secy. Smith, Feb. 14, 1808, in *ibid.*, XI, 439–440.

50. Jefferson to Gallatin, March 30, 1808, in *Writings of Gallatin*, I, 379–380.

51. Jefferson to Secy. Crowninshield, July 16, 1808, in Lipscomb, XII, 93. A few days earlier, Jefferson had notified Gallatin that both the Secretaries of Navy and War, knowing "our extreme anxiety to give a full effect to the important experiment of the embargo, at any expense within the bounds of reason," would therefore, on Gallatin's application, "yield the aid of their departments without waiting the delay of consulting me." July 12, 1808, in *ibid.*, pp. 82–83.

52. Gallatin to Jefferson, May 28, 1808, in *Writings of Gallatin*, I, 393.

53. Jefferson to Dearborn, July 18, 1808, in Lipscomb, XII, 102.

54. Jennings, *American Embargo*, pp. 115–116.

55. Jefferson to Dearborn, Aug. 9, 1808, in Lipscomb, XII, 119.

56. Jefferson to Crowninshield, Aug. 9, in *ibid.*, p. 121.

57. Gallatin to Jefferson, Aug. 9, 1808, in *Writings of Gallatin*, I, 403.

58. *Ibid.*, pp. 403–404.

59. Sears, *Jefferson and the Embargo*, pp. 93–94.

60. Jefferson to Tompkins, Aug. 15, 1808, in Lipscomb, XII, 132–133.

61. Jefferson to Gallatin, Aug. 15, in *ibid.*, p. 133.

62. Gallatin to Jefferson, Aug. 17, 1808, in *Writings of Gallatin*, I, 406.

63. Tompkins to Jefferson, Aug. 22, 1808, quoted in Sears, *Jefferson and the Embargo*, p. 94.

64. Gallatin to Jefferson, July 29, 1808, in *Writings of Gallatin*, I, 397.

65. Gallatin to Jefferson, Aug. 19, 1808, in *ibid.*, p. 407.

66. Jefferson to Gen. Wilkinson, Aug. 30, 1808, in Lipscomb, XII, 155.

67. *Ibid.*

68. Gallatin to Jefferson, Sept. 14, 1808, in *Writings of Gallatin*, I, 417.

69. *History of the U.S.*, IV, 273.

SIX. ANY MEANS TO THE END: THE EMBARGO, II

1. Gallatin to Jefferson, July 29, 1808, in *Writings of Gallatin*, I, 396–399.

2. *Ibid.*, p. 398.

3. Jefferson to James Brown, Oct. 27, 1808, in Lipscomb, XII, 183.

4. Adams, *History of the U.S.*, IV, 262.

5. Jefferson to Gallatin, Aug. 11, 1808, in Lipscomb, XII, 122.

6. Jefferson to Gallatin, Dec. 28, 1808, in *ibid.*, p. 221.

7. Gallatin to Jefferson, Dec. 28, 1808, in *Writings of Gallatin*, I, 447.

8. Act of April 25, 1808, sec. 11, in *Annals of Congress*, 10th Cong., 1st sess., p. 2873.

9. Jefferson to Gallatin, May 6, 1808, in Lipscomb, XII, 52.

10. Treasury Dept. Circular, May 6, 1808, in *The Embargo Laws* (Printed by Cushing and Belcher, Boston, 1809), pp. 19–20. This little book is a handy compilation of the various embargo acts, treasury circulars, the proceedings in *Gilchrist v. The Collector*, and the various French and British decrees.

11. *Gilchrist, and others v. The Collector of the Port of Charleston*, May 28, 1808, in *The Embargo Laws*, pp. 23–25.

12. *Ibid.*, pp. 25–27. The case is officially reported in 10 Fed. Cases 355 (C.C. Dist. of S. Car., 1808), case no. 5420.

13. See Charles Warren, *The Supreme Court in United States History* (Boston, 1923, 3 vols.), I, 326–328.

14. Jefferson to Pinckney, July 18, 1808, in Lipscomb, XII, 102–104.

15. "Letter from the Attorney General to the President of the United States, relative to the proceedings of the Circuit Court of South Carolina in the case of The Resource," 10 Fed. Cases 357–359.

16. Press quotations are from Warren, *Supreme Court,* I, 331–332.

17. For Johnson's reply to Rodney, see Warren, *Supreme Court,* I, 335, and Donald G. Morgan, *Justice William Johnson, The First Dissenter* (Columbia, S.C., 1954), pp. 63–65. The reply itself is reprinted in full in 10 Fed. Cases 359–366.

18. The facts of the case are taken from the report in *U.S. v. Hoxie,* case no. 15,407, in 26 Fed. Cases (C.C. Dist. of Vt., 1808) 379–403, and Sherman R. Moulton, "A Vermont Treason Trial," Vermont Bar Association, *Proceedings,* 29 (1935):135–136.

19. Jennings, *American Embargo,* pp. 115–116.

20. Jefferson to Gallatin, July 29, 1808, in Lipscomb, XII, 109.

21. Jefferson to Tompkins, Aug. 15, 1808, in *ibid.*, p. 133.

22. See Homer Cummings and Carl McFarland, *Federal Justice: Chapters in the History of Justice and the Federal Executive* (New York, 1937), p. 68; Warren, *Supreme Court,* I, 352; and Moulton, "A Vermont Treason Trial," p. 136.

23. Jefferson to Gallatin, Sept. 9, 1808, in Lipscomb, XII, 160.

24. *U.S. v. Hoxie,* case no. 15,407, in 26 Fed. Cases 397–403 (C.C. Dist. of Vt., 1808). Quotations of Livingston's opinion are from this source.

25. Justice Livingston also noted that the insurrectionists of 1798, Fries, Mitchel, and Vigol, who had been convicted for treason, were pardoned by President Adams. Adams' strict views of treason contrast sharply with Jefferson's in 1807–08. When Fries and his associates, under sentence of death, appealed to Adams for a pardon, he requested the advice of his cabinet on the following questions: "Is it clear beyond all reasonable doubt that the crime of which they stand convicted, amounts to a levying of war against the United States, or, in other words, to treason? . . . Is there not great danger in establishing such a construction of treason, as may be applied to every sudden, ignorant, inconsiderate heat, among a part of the people, wrought up by political

disputes, and personal or party animosities?" The members of the cabinet voted unanimously against pardons, but Adams pardoned all three prisoners anyway. He thought that the men should not have been indicted for any crime higher than riot, aggravated by rescue. "My judgment," he later wrote, "was clear, that their crime did not amount to treason. They had been guilty of high handed riot and rescue, attended with circumstances hot, rash, violent, and dangerous, but all these did not amount to treason." John Adams, *Works; with a Life of the Author,* ed. by Charles Francis Adams (Boston, 1850–1856, 10 vols.), IX, 58; X, 154.

26. Burlington *Centinel,* Nov. 4, 1808, quoted in Moulton, "A Vermont Treason Trial," p. 140.

27. Jefferson to M. Letue, Nov. 8, 1808, in Lipscomb, XII, 191.

28. *U.S. v. The William,* case no. 16,700, in 28 Fed. Cases 614 (C.C. Dist. of Mass., Oct. 1808). See also Francis Blake, *An Examination of the Constitutionality of the Embargo Laws . . . to Which Is Added the Opinion Pronounced by the Court* (Worcester, Mass., 1808), pp. 35f.

29. See the discussion in Warren, *Supreme Court,* I, 343–348.

30. Gallatin to Jefferson, Sept. 2, 1808, in *Writings of Gallatin,* I, 414. See also *ibid.,* p. 427.

31. On Blake, see Levy, *Legacy of Suppression,* pp. 210–211, 268.

32. Jefferson to Madison, Oct. 15, 1810, in Ford, IX, 283.

33. Jefferson to Gallatin, Oct. 25, 1808, in *Writings of Gallatin,* I, 420.

34. Gallatin to Giles, Nov. 24, 1808, in *ibid.,* p. 428.

35. For Jefferson's view on this point, see his letter to Gallatin, Dec. 7, 1808, in Lipscomb, XII, 209.

36. Gallatin to Giles, Nov. 24, 1808, in *Writings of Gallatin,* I, 431.

37. *Ibid.,* pp. 431–434. Gallatin's letter to Giles is also reprinted in the *Annals of Congress,* 10th Cong., 2nd sess., pp. 232–236.

38. *Annals of Congress,* 10th Cong., 2nd sess., p. 312.

39. *Ibid.,* p. 249.

40. *Ibid.,* p. 931.

41. *Ibid.,* pp. 246, 254, 292–294, 935–936, 983, 998–1000, 1012–1015.

42. *Ibid.,* pp. 1024, 1798–1804.

43. Jefferson to Madison, March 15, 1789, in Boyd, XIV, 661. The "Memorial and remonstrance" against the Fifth Embargo Act by the citizens of the third ward of New York City is an excellent statement that is in many respects analogous to the famed Ken-

tucky Resolutions of 1798. The same libertarian spirit and profession of concern for constitutional principles is evident. An extract of the long memorial, communicated to the House of Representatives on Feb. 6, 1809, is as follows: "That, in the exercise of the undoubted right of freemen, your memorialists approach the Legislature of the Union, to remonstrate against certain provisions of the late act for enforcing the embargo. At the same time, your memorialists offer to Congress a solemn assurance of their readiness to defend the rights of their country, not only against subjugation from abroad, but against usurpation and despotism at home. They are firmly attached to the Constitution and Union of these United States; and whenever no other alternative shall remain, they will be ready to vindicate, in arms, the cause of their country and of its liberties.

"Until now, it has been the boast of those who love this country and its political institutions, that we have a Government of laws, not of men; that our citizens are liable to punishment only upon judicial conviction of offences, not on suspicion; that no person can be deprived of life, liberty, or property, without due process of law; that the right of being secure against unreasonable searches, cannot be violated; that warrants cannot issue but upon probable cause, supported by oath or affirmation; and as the great bulwark of defence for all these rights, that the trial by jury shall be preserved. If principles, in their nature so original, and so necessarily interwoven with the fabric of every free Government, can need a formal sanction, it will be found in the letter of the fourth, fifth, and seventh amendments to the Constitution, and in the spirit of every part of that instrument.

"In the act against which your memorialists remonstrate, they see direct and palpable violations of these principles, in the following, among other particulars:

"That by this act, a citizen may be deprived of his property without process of law:

"That, by this act, a citizen may be deprived of his property at the caprice of individuals, not only when innocent of any offence, but of the intent to commit any:

"That by this act, a citizen may be deprived of his property without an offence committed, without proof, without trial, without judgment, without the benefit of a legal appeal against the injustice, and without remedy:

"That, by this act, our property is subjected to instructions from the President, which may be kept secret; which may be different for different classes of men; which may proceed from misinformation, or worse causes; and which may be partial, arbitrary, and oppressive:

"That, by this act, our property is placed under the discretion of officers of the revenue, with more than judicial powers, who, yet, are not sworn as judges, nor liable to impeachment as such; nor independent in office, nor presumed to be learned in the laws, nor bound to examine facts, or hear the accused:

"That, by this act, our property is subjected to seizures, which may proceed, not only from mistake or false information, but from private malice, party animosity, or other corrupt motives:

"That, by this act, the military power is introduced into the execution of municipal law before any resistance made, and when there is neither rebellion, war, nor danger of invasion:

"That, by this act, we are subjected to vexatious searches and intrusions, without probable cause supported by oath or affirmation:

"That, by this act, belief of guilt is taken for guilt itself, and, without the forms of law, is punished accordingly:

"That, by this act, we are subjected to secret and odious inquisitions, inasmuch as, when informed against, we have no means of knowing the accusation, or of being confronted with the witnesses, or of having a public trial:

"That, by this act, new conditions are annexed to bonds already given, and some of these conditions impossible to be performed:

"That this act appears intended to bar the legal remedies for seizures, and other wrongs which may be most oppressive; and, instead of the law of the land, our undoubted and hitherto undisputed birthright, it refers us, for redress, to a petition, a summary hearing, and the final discretion of a district judge:

"That, by this act, the Legislative, Judicial, and Executive powers, are vested in one man; which is despotism.

"The intention of your memorialists has been to confine themselves, in this remonstrance, chiefly to the objections of unconstitutionality; but they presume to notice some of the other particulars in which they conceive the act to be oppressive to the citizens, and dangerous to public liberty . . .

"Another effect, not less to be deplored, is, that this act, like all arbitrary powers, is calculated to infest society with spies and informers. It will multiply fees, and the exactions of office, encourage prosecutions, and enrich a host, not only of spies and informers, but of collectors, surveyors, tide-waiters, and other custom house officers, district attorneys, marshals, clerks, and their subordinate agents, who will fatten upon the public distress . . .

"Such an act is not more a violation of the express words, and whole scope of our written Constitution, than it is an attack upon those fundamental principles of civil liberty, which, anterior to all charters of rights and powers, form the basis of every social compact." *Annals of Congress,* 10th Cong., 2nd sess., app., pp. 1777–1780. The views expressed in the memorial, though only those of a besieged political minority, doubtlessly based on economic grievances that are masked by constitutional arguments, are as principled as the Kentucky Resolutions of 1798 and as well founded.

44. *Annals of Congress,* 10th Cong., 2nd sess., p. 946.

45. *Ibid.,* pp. 950–960.

46. *Ibid.,* pp. 1192–1229.

47. *Ibid.,* pp. 1193–1194. Jefferson alluded to this bill in his private correspondence without explicitly indicating his position on it. He certainly did not disclose any opposition to it, for he promised a commission in the regular army to a friend's son if the bill passed. He remarked, however, that the volunteers would not be called upon for active duty "till war is declared, or inevitable." Jefferson to Capt. Armistead T. Mason of the Virginia militia, Feb. 3, 1809, in Lipscomb, XII, 246–247. The bill before the House did not include a provision restricting the active duty of the 50,000 volunteers to time of war or its imminence. It provided for discretionary powers in the President regarding the assignment of the army to active duty and for the encampment of the men for a period of thirty days out of the year, at a cost of $2,100,000.

48. Jefferson to Thomas Mann Randolph, Feb. 7, 1809, in Lipscomb, XII, 248.

49. Jefferson to Dupont de Nemours, March 2, 1809, in *ibid.,* pp. 259–260.

SEVEN. ON GUARD AGAINST POLITICAL HERESIES: OF HUME AND THE UNIVERSITY OF VIRGINIA

1. Jefferson to Horatio G. Spafford, March 17, 1814, in E. Millicent Sowerby, ed., *Catalog of the Library of Thomas Jefferson* (Washington, 1952–1959, 5 vols.), II, 229.

2. Jefferson to Madison, Feb. 17, 1826, in Lipscomb, XVI, 156.

3. Tucker, ed., *Blackstone's Commentaries: with notes of reference, to the Constitution and Laws, of the Federal Government of the United States . . . and of the Commonwealth of Virginia. With an appendix to each volume, containing short tracts upon such subjects as appeared necessary to form a connected view of the Laws of Virginia, as a Member of the Federal Union* (Phila-

delphia, 1803, 5 vols.). Tucker's edition was recommended by Jefferson on his reading lists. See, for example, Jefferson to John Minor, Aug. 30, 1814, in Ford, IX, 483.

4. Jefferson to John Norvell, June 11, 1807, in Lipscomb, XI, 223–224. Baxter was an English radical of the late eighteenth century.

5. Jefferson to Duane, Aug. 12, 1810, in Lipscomb, XII, 405–407.

6. See letters by Jefferson to John Minor, Aug. 30, 1814, in Ford, IX, 483; to John Adams, Nov. 25, 1816, in Lipscomb, XV, 86–87; to Mathew Carey, Nov. 22, 1818, in Sowerby, ed., *Catalog,* I, 177; to Thomas W. White, Feb. 5, 1820, in *ibid.,* p. 178; to John Cartwright, June 5, 1824, in Lipscomb, XVI, 44; and to [George Washington Lewis], Oct. 25, 1825, in *ibid.,* pp. 124–128. Lewis, whom Lipscomb does not name as recipient of the letter, has been identified by other editors.

7. Jefferson to Mathew Carey, Nov. 22, 1818, in Sowerby, ed., *Catalog,* I, 177.

8. Jefferson to White, Feb. 5, 1820, and Dec. 11, 1823, in Sowerby, ed., *Catalog,* I, 178.

9. Jefferson to George W. Lewis, Oct. 25, 1825, in Lipscomb, XVI, 126, 128. In this letter to Carey, Jefferson declared that when the student who reads Hume "becomes a statesman, he will become also the tory of our constitution, disposed to monarchise the government, by strengthening the Executive, and weakening the popular branch, and by drawing the municipal administration of the states into the vortex of general authority." Nov. 22, 1818, in Sowerby, ed., *Catalog,* I, 177.

10. Enactment of the Board of Visitors of the University of Virginia, April 7, 1824, in Lipscomb, XIX, 443. Roy J. Honeywell, *The Educational Work of Thomas Jefferson* (Cambridge, Mass., 1931), is a useful introduction to Jefferson's work in connection with the University of Virginia.

11. Jefferson to Spencer Roane, June 27, 1821, in Lipscomb, XV, 328.

12. Jefferson to William B. Giles, Dec. 26, 1825, in *ibid.,* XVI, 146–148.

13. *Ibid.,* p. 151.

14. Jefferson to Thomas Cooper, Aug. 14, 1820, in *ibid.,* XV, 264.

15. Jefferson to Joseph C. Cabell, Jan. 31, 1821, in *ibid.,* p. 311.

16. Jefferson to James Breckinridge, Feb. 15, 1821, in *ibid.,* p. 315.

17. Jefferson to Madison, Feb. 17, 1826, in *ibid.*, XVI, 156.

18. Jefferson to William Short, Jan. 8, 1825, in *ibid.*, p. 96.

19. *Ibid.* See also Jefferson to William Johnson, June 12, 1823, in *ibid.*, XV, 443–444, and to Henry Lee, Aug. 10, 1824, in *ibid.*, XVI, 74.

20. Jefferson to Cabell, Feb. 3, 1825, in *ibid.*, XVI, 104. The same letter and an almost identical letter to Madison, Feb. 1, 1825, is in the appendix to the extremely interesting essay by Arthur Bestor on "Thomas Jefferson and the Freedom of Books," which appears in Bestor, *et al.*, *Three Presidents and Their Books* (Urbana, Ill., 1955). Bestor's essay expresses a quite different viewpoint from mine and is therefore recommended to readers. While Bestor is by no means uncritical and states his disagreement with the apologetics characterizing Koch's *Jefferson and Madison*, pp. 275–279, he attempts, unconvincingly in my opinion, to defend Jefferson. See Bestor, pp. 24–35. The appendix to his essay, pp. 39–44, includes the exact text of the letters from Jefferson to Cabell and Madison, of Feb. 1 and 3, 1825, their replies, and the relevant extract from the minutes of the Board of Visitors, March 4, 1825.

21. Madison to Samuel H. Smith, Nov. 4, 1826, in Hunt, ed., *Writings of Madison*, IX, 259.

22. Madison to Jefferson, Feb. 17, 1825, quoted in Koch, *Jefferson and Madison*, p. 275, citing Madison Papers, Library of Congress.

23. See above, footnote 25 of Chapter Three.

24. Madison to Jefferson, Feb. 8, 1825, in Hunt, ed., *Writings of Madison*, IX, 218–220. Also in Bestor, *Three Presidents*, app., pp. 41–42.

25. *Ibid.*

26. Minutes of the Board of Visitors of the University of Virginia, March 4, 1825, in Lipscomb, XIX, 460–461. Also in Bestor, *Three Presidents*, app., pp. 43–44.

27. Jefferson to William Roscoe, Dec. 27, 1820, in Lipscomb, XV, 303.

EIGHT. JEFFERSON AS A LIBERTARIAN: CONCLUSIONS ON THE DARKER SIDE

1. *Memoirs of John Quincy Adams, Comprising Portions of His Diary from 1795 to 1848*, ed. by Charles Francis Adams (Philadelphia, 1874–1877, 12 vols.), entries of Jan. 11 and 12, 1831, VIII, 270–272.

2. "Address at Dedication of the Thomas Jefferson Memorial,

Washington, D.C.," April 13, 1943, quoted in Francis Coleman Rosenberger, ed., *Jefferson Reader: A Treasury of Writings About Thomas Jefferson* (New York, 1953), pp. 246–247.

3. Rich, *Presidents and Civil Disorder*, p. 5.

4. James Morton Smith, *Freedom's Fetters: The Alien and Sedition Laws and American Civil Liberties* (Ithaca, N.Y., 1956), pp. 297–298, 299–300.

5. "My Grandfather, Mr. Jefferson," in Rosenberger, ed., *Jefferson Reader*, pp. 65–66.

6. Jefferson to Roger C. Weightman, June 24, 1826, in Lipscomb, XVI, 182.

7. See Jefferson to Gallatin, Sept. 9, 1808, in Lipscomb, XII, 161. See also, in *ibid.*, pp. 86, 95–96, 103, 111, 128, 130, 145–146, 169.

8. Dixon Wecter, "Thomas Jefferson, The Gentle Radical," in Rosenberger, ed., *Jefferson Reader*, p. 312, reprinting an essay from Wecter's *The Hero in America: A Chronicle of Hero-Worship* (New York, 1941).

9. Jefferson himself expressed a similar opinion in a letter to William Duane, the eminent Republican publisher. In the course of the letter Jefferson discoursed on the need for sensitivity to the possibility that one's own political judgments may be wrong when in conflict with those of the majority of one's party. He spoke of his own fallibility, the spirit of compromise, and the attribute of self-distrust. But the purpose of the letter was to bring Duane back to the Republican fold. He had been running editorials criticizing Madison's Administration, and Jefferson's remarks were calculated to discourage Duane from expressing independent judgment. The entire lecture on self-distrust and compromise was a tactical device to restore party unity by ridding the Republican press of dissent. Jefferson was scarcely admitting that he was or had ever been wrong; he was trying to convince Duane that he was wrong. See Jefferson to Duane, April 30, 1811, in Lipscomb, XIII, 47–52.

10. Jefferson to Edward Livingston, April 4, 1824, in *ibid.*, XVI, 25.

11. *Ibid.* See also Jefferson to William B. Giles, Dec. 26, 1825, in *ibid.*, p. 148.

12. Jefferson to Henry Lee, May 8, 1825, in *ibid.*, p. 118.

13. Felix Frankfurter, *Of Law and Men: Papers and Addresses of Felix Frankfurter*, ed. by Philip Elman (New York, 1956), "The Permanence of Jefferson," p. 232.

Index

Index

Index

Index